Dedicated to

My mother, Mrs. Teena Virk
who has been my inspiration, my true soul mate and
the strongest guiding force in making me discover
my true human potential
&

To my father Mr. Ravinder Singh Virk
who has been the balancing factor in my life,
for his constant support and stable practical advice.

Mom... Dad
I could never have done this without both of you.

Acknowledgements

I would sincerely like to thank all those who have been part of this amazing journey and who believed in my vision, especially Dr Jaideep Chadha for his consistent and patient guidance at every step.

I would like to thank Mr. Rohit Gupta for putting his faith in me by publishing my dream work.

My sincere gratitude to guruji Shiv Malhotra for having taught me this form of art and bringing me in touch with my true calling.

My heartfelt thanks to Gulshan Virk for her unending support in helping me spread my message, to Ishwinder Jauhar for his brilliant photographic work and to Seema Gupta for her skilled editing. Special thanks to my students as well who inspired me to write this book.

Contents

Preface

$\mathscr{I}$ must say it surely feels strange being on the other side of the fence having gone through the apprehensions, the doubts, the cynicism. Well, we all develop such feelings before we plunge in or take a leap into the unknown. Those of you who have already tasted the fruits of this tree might just identify with this feeling at a much more personal level. This is precisely where I step in to help you unravel and embrace the much hyped about **Yoga boom**. All you need before we start this awesome journey is a little faith and fluidity. Freedom from all your pre-conceived notions that you might have formed from new theories, your existing mode of practice or exodus of information floating around will also come handy.

Let's take it right from the start. What is the first thing that comes to your mind when someone asks you about yoga?

For a layman, I bet it is all about twisting around in awkward positions probably getting entangled till a point of no return and breathing so hard that your lungs might be at risk of bursting out. And, how can we miss the oh-so-predictable saffron *chogas* and *khadi jholas*? For those of you who are a tad bit more familiar with the *asanas*, *pranayama* routine, I might have a surprise in store for you as we move from merely scratching the surface to the very depths of this abysmal form of art. You must be now thinking, 'yeah we've heard that presumptuous statement before', but stop right there. Let's rewind and replay as we begin to redefine yoga. The word *YOGA* itself refers to **discipline**.... This discipline is not of the regimented effort-oriented kind, which is acquired by merely following clock and calendar. It is rather of a rhythmic soulful nature that can only ensue from balancing out all the extremes from your mind body and soul.

Sounds rather far-fetched but I assure you it is as simple as you choose to make it. All we need to start with is your mind. Trust me, it is not a **state of mind** lecture yet again. Here I choose to be a tad unpredictable and so it is the **state of being** that I want to introduce you to. Okay, so let's break it down to the basics.

I want you to ask yourself honestly that how often you, in a given situation, just allow yourself to flow with the tide without struggling to steer the path. If you look deep inside, you would realise that we humans believe that we have an innate ability to control. Ironically some of us gradually do become aware in the course of time. Nevertheless, most of us choose to remain oblivious to the reality, that events in our iives are governed by a pre-ordained nature of destiny that each one of us is born with. Simply recognising this reality and submitting to it is what I define as the **state of being**.

I agree it does not come naturally which is evident by the chaotic times we all live in. But remember each one of us, at one point of time or the other, is an active contributor to this circle of chaos. Thus we all must stop and make a choice, rather make a commitment to ourselves, to put an end to this discord arising from the discrepancy between the ways we think, feel and eventually act. This is precisely where the role of yoga begins. It aims at simply bridging the gap between what we, as individuals, are capable of becoming and what we, paradoxically, end up making of ourselves. This might be in terms of the thoughts we nurture, or our physical health, or our spiritual state.

Yoga is the tool which would help you peel back all the layers of pretence. It would also make you break through all those barriers and bondages that keep you from discovering your true human potential, helping you make peace with who you are as an individual — totally unique with your own share of luck, wisdom and valour. It is a facet of yoga which is given the least bit of emphasis by majority of practitioners. However, it is the most crucial factor in understanding the real essence of yoga. I am quite certain that most of you already practising the art of yoga would have seldom touched upon this aspect, especially in the beginning stages. But, here I take the liberty to reverse the order.

So all we need to start with is to work on the level of awareness that each one of us possesses, but sometimes lose touch with getting swept away by the tide of life, in our mundane routines, mechanical chores, duties, obligations... the list is never-ending. So all you need to do is to extract those little minuscule moments from your busy schedules to just be yourself. Do nothing more than just spend some time with your innermost secret thoughts, beliefs, aspirations, dreams, desires and simply *float away*. Now I know it sounds pretty nutty. But believe me, there is no greater **HIGH** than being able to **unplug and unwind** making a deep and honest connection with your true self.

— **Meghna Virk Bains**

Evolution of Yoga

In order to get a holistic view of any discipline, it is extremely important to trace back its origin and evolution. It is this very trip back in history that actually helps you rediscover the authentic nature of things as they existed in their nascent stage, and how with time they acquired their present form and flavour. To trace the historical background of yoga systematically, we shall classify it into four distinct time periods — Pre-classical, Classical, Post-classical and Modern.

Pre-Classial

The origin of this ancient art can be traced back to the Indus Valley Civilisation in northern India over 5000 years ago. The word 'yoga' finds its reference in the oldest Indian literature, the *Rig Veda*, a collection of texts containing hymns and rituals followed by Brahmin priests. Yoga was slowly refined and developed by these priests, who documented their practices and beliefs in the Upanishads. The Upanishads preached the sacrifice of ego through self-knowledge, action and wisdom.

The Classical Period

This period saw the systematic presentation of yoga through the emergence of Patanjali's *yogasutras*. Patanjali is considered to be the father of yoga and his *sutras* form the fundamental basis of all its styles. These *sutras* written some time in the 2nd century organised yoga into an 'eight-limbed path'. It comprised the steps and stages towards obtaining *samadhi* or enlightenment.

Post-Classical Period

A few centuries after Patanjali, yoga-masters created a system of practices designed to rejuvenate body and prolong life. They rejected teachings of the ancient Vedas and embraced physical body as the means to achieve enlightenment. They developed 'Tantric Yoga'. It was a set of radical techniques to cleanse the body and facilitate the mind to break through the fetters that keep us fastened to our physical existence. This exploration of physical-spiritual connection and body-centred practices led to the creation of 'Hatha Yoga'.

Modern Period

In the late 1800s and early 1900s, yoga began its journey westwards. Hatha Yoga was strongly promoted in India with the lifelong work of **T. Krisnamacharya**. He travelled throughout the country demonstrating the yoga poses and opened the first Hatha Yoga School. The three disciples of Krishnamacharya, **B.K.S. Iyengar**, **T.K.V. Desikachar** and **Pattabhi Jois**, carried his legacy forward.

Since then many more western and Indian teachers have emerged, popularising Hatha Yoga which now has many different schools or styles. All these styles emphasise upon the many different aspects of the practice revolving essentially around the main philosophy of yoga, that is, mind, body and spirit are all one. Thus no clear demarcation is possible between them.

Five Basic Steps in Yoga

*N*ow there might be a question lingering in your mind (an organ I definitely feel we all can so happily do without). Why would anyone in his sane mind choose to spend valuable moments out of their 'time is money' schedule just to gaze into the empty spaces? Who would make attempt to connect with some godforsaken 'inner true self' which perhaps you did not even know existed up to this moment of time? And how the hell is that supposed to make any iota of a difference to your seemingly normal life!

Well, this is precisely the point I am attempting to drive home. Haven't we all reached a stage where it has become too much to ask to touch our own depths? Don't you feel that we all have touched such a shallow level of our existence where all that seems to matter is the car we drive, the locality we can afford to reside in, the number of prestigious club memberships we have and so on? Do you really believe that this is what defines your purpose in this one and only journey of life?

It is never too late to learn, neither is there any harm in learning how to live as long as you are alive. Thus, I suggest it is time we take a step forward opening up our senses, making them more alive to plunge in to awareness. The concept of awareness, as I feel, is of immense value. This is precisely because it is a journey you make inwards. It helps you expose the depths till you touch your own core without getting trapped in the irreversibility of past and the inevitability of future.

So you neither take a reverse gear nor try to over speed. You rather start cherishing and absorbing the value of the present day and moment, enjoying them here and now.

Now, before you lose all your patience and toss this work of art away, let me come to the point. For accomplishing this seemingly complicated task, we need to turn back to the art of yoga. Yoga is the tool that would help you rediscover the power of your own senses. It is a process that essentially involves **FIVE** basic steps that enable you to acquire a heightened sense of perception, physical health, mental peace and spiritual enlightenment. So here we go, fasten your seatbelts.

▼ The very first step deals with the *'ASANAS'*. You must have heard this word before in relation to yoga but this time let us try not to be so technical about it. All it is about is just the art of holding a certain pose, since the literal meaning of *'asana'* is seat. When I say 'holding', you must remember it does not involve any effort whatsoever, which is usually what we all as beginners try to do — push our body beyond the comfort zone just for the sake of taking a particular position. Yoga is neither an exercise nor a gymnastic competition. It simply boils down to the level of stability and placidity you can slowly and steadily induce into your postures. Yoga helps you open up your ligaments by stretching and strengthening them, activating your energy centres (we shall discuss them a little later) and stimulating the blood circulation in your limbs, joints and muscles.

Most of the time, we are so engrossed in our routine events and chores of lives that very seldom do we actually bother about simple basics, like a good healthy posture. Yes, I know we were all pulled up by our parents and teachers as sloppy kids in school when we walked with that 'I don't care' hunchy walk and lanky posture. But remember, it is really never too late for amends. So, if you have the basic ability to modify and become a tad bit more conscious about your posture then that is evidence enough that you are ready to take on the challenge. All you need to do even as you read these lines, is to put the book down and straighten up your back and neck. Remember, the spinal cord is your lifeline!

Just be at ease and take pride in maintaining a proper posture at all times. You will be amazed how much of a positive difference it makes. It not only affects the way your body starts functioning but also the way people perceive your confidence levels by just observing your body language. So the next time you walk into a room full of people, just hold your head high and stride forward.

Even as you practise *asanas* on a daily basis, make sure you let the benefits creep in slowly and steadily into your entire lifestyle. Make no watertight compartments by maintaining just the great postures and then letting it all go out of the window the moment you walk out.

▼ Step number two is one of my favourite and definitely the most cardinal aspect of yoga — *'PRANAYAMA'*. Once again I would advice you to leave your pre-fixed modes and methods behind and just flow along. That is precisely what this concept requires — a cool, calm, uncluttered state of being.

Let me clearly explain the literal meaning of the word *pranayama* by breaking it into two parts. *Prana* quite simply can be translated as the energy force that sustains your life. *Yama* refers to mastering the art of channelising this energy positively. This is possible only by means of a thriving system of breathing well.

The basic idea is to increase the intake of fresh and oxygenated air. So it is the extension of our breathing passage which is extremely crucial. You will be amazed to know that this passage that I am referring to extends from the base of our abdomen right up to the top of our head. I understand it is really hard to conceive. You might already be getting breathless, but just hold on a little longer and let me help you breathe easy. Once you become aware of this passage, you can work on increasing the depths of inhaling and exhaling steadily and patiently.

Contrary to popular belief, it is not just enough to breathe in deep and long, which is what some of you might already be following. Breathing out as deep as you breathe in is of equal importance. In fact the actual ratio one must strive to achieve is a 1:2. The amount of time you take to breathe in should be twice of what you take while breathing out.

Be very cautious and patient because it is not something you would achieve overnight. It is something that would slowly grow on you and then become an integral part of your system.

Now the logical question that must be flooding you at this point of time would probably be — why does one need to apply such precision and technique for something as easy as breathing?

Well, thanks to our technology-driven high-flier lifestyles, even breathing comes at a cost nowadays. Since most of us are so addicted to our artificially modified environments of air conditioners (in summers) and heaters (in winters) right from the workplace, to our cars and homes, we hardly leave any room for fresh air. Not that I expect you to take drastic unsustainable steps like banning the use of air conditioners or heaters completely. All I ask of you is to take out just half an hour or at the least 10 minutes to breathe deep in order to cleanse your system. While you indulge in this practice, make sure you use your lungs to their optimum capacity and breathe out as effectively to complete the energy cycle.

Thus **purity of breathing** forms the foundation stone of yoga. It is the coordination of *asanas* with breathing that lends real essence and meaning to this traditional art.

▾ Moving on to step three, we talk about '*MUDRAS*'. It is an aspect related to yoga, which I personally feel, is beginning to fade-out owing to the transition in the mindset of new generation. These days, we witness power-packed and vigorous forms of yoga being taught and followed to keep pace with the fast, modern lifestyles. Those of you into the groove of this hip and happening yoga, ought to pay double attention to this point.

Essentially *mudras* refer to the grace and beauty with which a particular movement is performed or a position is held. This concept lends an **artistic flavour to yoga**. My aim here is not to discourage you from keeping up your regimen of gyming or working out. The idea is just to make you clearly see how yoga exists as a form of art as opposed to merely being a form of exercise.

I am quite familiar with most people's obsession with their workout and gym. They take them to be the only remedy for all their disorders. However, such people often forget that the physical disorders that they want to eradicate so desperately have their roots deep at their mental level. So the fact remains that they often find quick-fix solutions to control the superficial problems. However, the healing that has to take place deep inside their body is something that is often overlooked. Thus, in yoga, great emphasis is laid upon the quality of gestures while you perform an *asana* or even *pranayama*.

Let me exemplify the **meditation mudra** wherein you touch your thumb with the index finger. On the face of it, it might look pointless; but if you notice whenever you are in an angry mood, filled with aggression and egotism, it is the index finger that you often use for accusations. You rarely greet lovingly by pointing the index finger at each other. So the mere bending of this finger signifies letting go of all your negative egocentric vibes and feelings. Also the *mudra*, in turn, becomes a constant reminder for you to be more humble. This is what forms the strong and stable base for you to meditate upon. The slower and gentler the pace, the greater is the absorption by your system and senses of all the benefits of *asanas* and *pranayama*. So whenever you intend to take on to yoga, remember it is not the pace, but the grace that does the trick.

▼ We have talked about the significance and the role that physical postures play in purifying the breathing energy. We have also touched upon the importance of maintaining a certain level of grace in our gestures. So now, I feel, is the time to move on to the next step, which is called *'SHATKARMA'*. For that, it would be advisable if you to revisit all the steps once again. That is because the literal meaning of *shatkarma* is 'internal cleansing' which is precisely what we are trying to achieve at each and every step. Now you see whether it is an *asana* which you perform while lying down, sitting or standing or it is *pranayama* or *mudras*, we are basically aiming at cleansing the digestive tract, draining out the stiffness from the spine, joints, muscles, ligaments, and unclogging the breathing passage. So on observing closely, you would find that it is the value of internal cleansing which we intend to focus on consistently. It is the perfect balance and coordination between the physical movements, breathing, grace and cleansing that we are constantly striving to achieve. All these factors collectively make yoga an **indispensable tool for living a complete and holistic life at all levels.**

▼ Finally we top this sumptuous recipe, with the fifth and final step, *'RELAXATION'*. Now this, I am sure, each one of you feels is something that requires no further explanation. You are in for bit of a surprise; ironically it is one step that beats all the others in terms of actual implementation. So please, do not take it for granted. It is an art that certainly needs mastering. Most people, as I have personally observed, struggle hard with this concept of just hanging loose, letting go of all their problems, tensions, hassles, and disengaging themselves from their hectic routines while performing their yoga. Remember it is not enough to just master and perfect the moves and gestures. It is all the more important to let the 'state of being' become an actual way of living for you. You have to be ready to make an honest, sincere and complete surrender of your ego and scepticism. Only then you would be able to fully absorb all that is positive, good and healthy for your mind, body and soul.

To put it in simpler terms, you need to learn to *'go with the flow'*.

The Seven Chakras

Before we move any further, let me discuss another crucial aspect of the conceptual base of yoga with you, which is *'THE CHAKRAS'*. Most of you while practising the art might have overlooked this significant correlation that exists between these seven vital energy centres and yoga. To understand this concept, you need to sharpen your visualising and mental perception skills because we generally envision *chakras* as 'the whirling disks of light'. These *chakras* are constantly running through our system and emanating their energy into our senses. Also, each *chakra* is associated with a specific colour.

The *chakras* start from the base of your spine and spiral right up to the top of your head. As I describe each one to you, my attempt shall be to help you correlate them with a specific spiritual, emotional, psychological and physical issue that governs your mind, body and soul. The purpose behind this seemingly arduous task is to help you balance out each of these energy centres through a series of *asanas, pranayama, mudras, shatkarma* and overall relaxation. This would eventually facilitate the enhancement of your conscious awareness and physical well-being. Remember it all revolves around learning your **'body language'**, so let us get started.

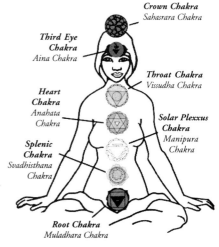

The seven energy chakra in human body

▼ The first *chakra* is the *'MULADHARA'* located at the base of your spine. Its colour is red and it ropes in issues related to survival, stability and self-sufficiency. Now just stop for a while and analyse. It would not appear to be so complicated if you just learn to read the signs. It is the spine which forms the foundation of our survival. It provides utmost stability to our body structure enabling movements for performing our functions on a daily basis. As you attempt to invoke the dormant energy from this centre during any *asana*, simply repeat these words —

"May I be able to nourish and nurture myself, be grounded, stable and feel connected to the oneness of life!"

Trust me, as you repeat these words, the power of the energy-flow would literally begin to rush throughout your spine. These words are the verbal embodiment of power.

▼ The second *chakra*, the *'SVADHISTHANA'*, is located in the lower abdomen (between the belly button and pelvic bone). It is associated with orange colour. The issues related to this *chakra* include sexuality, creativity, relationships and emotions. Once again try to simply correlate the functions performed by each of your organs situated in the lower abdomen. You will be able to easily figure out how these issues emerge thereby. These are the words you must repeat while invoking the dormant energy in this centre —

"May I be at home and at ease with my body, and find balance in my relationships between myself and others!"

▼ The third *chakra*, *'MANIPURA'*, is located in the upper abdomen (between the belly button and bottom of rib cage). Its colour is yellow and it involves issues like personal power, self-esteem, wilfulness and energy. Remember the expression 'gut feeling' so commonly used by us! This is the centre from where that strong feeling of conviction flows. So this is what you need to say to yourself to enlighten this energy centre —

"May I be able to honour myself, be who I am in the world, and express that power without fear!"

▼ The fourth *chakra* '*ANAHATA*' located in the centre of your chest has the green colour. Issues associated with this centre are love, compassion, acceptance and trust. It will be very easy for you to relate to this *chakra* since most of us are pretty much in touch with our heart and that is where all these energies emanate from. Also, it is the *anahata* that is considered as the balance centre. This is because of its location right in the middle of all the *chakras* with three *chakras* below this point and three above it. Keeping this centre enlightened and activated is what eventually helps you strike the perfect balance between the way you think, feel and act. So keep these words in mind —

"May I be free, to feel my true feelings, desires and passions and be at home with my heart!"

▼ The fifth *chakra* '*VISSUDHA*' is located in the throat. Its colour is bright blue. Issues it governs include communication, inspiration, expression and faith. Keeping this centre enlightened guarantees the enhancement of your interactive skills and clarity of thoughts with equal clarity of expression. The words you must remember are —

"May I be able to express my feelings with ease, and be balanced between heart and mind!"

▼ The sixth *chakra* is '*AINA*'. It is located between the eyebrows just above the bridge of the nose. Its colour is indigo blue. The issues that emerge from this centre are psychological clarity, mental intelligence and intuition. No wonder the 'sixth sense' or what we mythologically refer to as 'the third eye' finds its location in this centre. To derive this clear perception, the words that must follow are —

"May I see and perceive clearly at every level, and seek only the truth!"

▼ The seventh *chakra* '*SAHASRARA*' commonly referred to as 'the thousand-petalled' has the colour violet. Issues it controls are devotion, selflessness and spiritual understanding. Let us just say that this final destination is our main control room. It keeps us functioning in perfect harmony and synchronisation, setting the rhythm of our life. These are the words that complement the synthesis that you will achieve at this level —

"May I have a clear and open connection with my spirit and live in the present moment!"

As you finish reading this section, just close your eyes and try to envision these seven 'energy disks' rotating throughout your system and senses. Feel them resonate their positive vibes in every nook and corner of your being, at the same time rejuvenating, refreshing, relaxing and re-igniting you.

Role of Yoga in Women's Life

I am quite certain that by now you must have figured out the basic concepts and tenets upon which yoga has been based as a discipline. As I try to break away from the humdrum mould that yoga is so often put into, let me begin with sharing with you my personal experience. Yoga has certainly played a vital role in my life as a woman.

It is a journey that I believe every woman is entitled to and must take. It would make sure that she does not lose track of her true self, and beliefs and values that she holds dear. We, women, always run at the risk of losing ourselves in the tide. This is because we are on a constant transitional journey, with our roles changing every moment, from daughters and sisters to daughters-in-law and wives to the noblest of them all — that of a mother. We are defined by the roles we fulfil each day in our lives. Yoga, I believe, is the tool that might make this strenuous journey a smooth sail for each one of you, provided you are ready to make the commitment to yourself.

This commitment that I am referring to is not just a physical level of discipline that allows you to take out that half an hour from your schedule. It also involves a certain degree of amendment in your mental attitude to be receptive enough to allow the experience to seep in, assimilate, and get absorbed through the body, mind and soul. Remember, yoga is not a mere means of exercise to shed those extra kilos. Once you comprehend this well, you can expect yoga to become a way of living for you. And trust me, that is the only way it can become worth pursuing!

I know it is getting a bit heavy to digest, so let us begin with a light warm-up first. Well, we all like to possess a toned up, sexy, slim, sultry figure. And mind you, it is *our* obsession so let us not blame men entirely for their imagination. I agree there is absolutely no harm whatsoever in harbouring such dreams. Just let them not turn into an all-consuming obsession in which all your energies, emotions, actions and reactions are governed purely by the way your physical appearance is.

See, I am not here to lecture you or redefine your lifestyles. My attempt is purely to make you realise your worth not only at a physical, but also mental, emotional and spiritual level. We, as women, have been created and blessed with such heightened levels of sensitivity, perception, emotion, expression, and creativity. So it becomes all the more imperative for us to spare a little time to rediscover the innate balance which so naturally exists in us. So trust me when I say, you have the ability, you have the excellence. All you need now is a little effort, to devote time to pamper yourself.

To begin with, all you need to do is make yourself conscious of the fact that there exist multitudinous similarities between you as a woman and yoga as an institution. So this journey that you are about to take on, might just turn out to be more of a **self-discovery** than about **yoga-discovery**. And that is exactly how I intend it to be — SO ENJOY THE RIDE...

Let us begin the journey by fixing certain **milestones** which will eventually lead us to our destination. These might be as follows:

1. *The Troublesome Teenage*
2. *The Transitional Twenties*
3. *The Whirling Working Years*
4. *The Moonlit Marriage Years*
5. *The Precarious Pregnancy*
6. *The Menacing Menopause*
7. *The Graceful Aging Years*

The main purpose behind this classification is to make it easier for you to decipher as to what yoga routine you should be following corresponding with a specific physical, mental and emotional stage. My aim is also to do away with the popular misconceptions that yoga is only beneficial if taken up at an early age. Yoga is all about learning your body language, for which the age is definitely not a criteria. Believe me, it is never too late to set the rhythm of your mind, body and soul right.

The Troublesome Teenage

Now do not take offence at being called 'the troublesome teens'. It is not you that I am referring to as the troublesome ones, but it is the issues that we, as girls, have to deal with. The issues involved are truly troublesome, beginning right from getting used to filling up of the body, to balancing out weight and height proportions, to dealing with pimples, to the menstruation cycles. And as if it were not enough trouble already, we also get burdened with getting the ace grades at school. Gosh, it is really a lot of pressure! And how can I forget to mention the 'figuring out what to wear' phenomenon that has become such a rage nowadays, adding additional pressure on the little ladies.

I must mention here that I myself was a troubled teenager when I decided to take-off on this amazing journey. The beginning months did seem like a self-imposed torture. It is just not easy to pull yourself up from a 'zero' level of discipline, where words like peace, health, spirituality and balance seem like wacky concepts, which add no meaning whatsoever to your ignorant world. It took me almost a whole year to break the ice and accept yoga as an indispensable part of my life, rather than being a mere time pass in summer vacations. For such a 'miracle' to happen, having an awesome guide is important. I was lucky to have guruji Shiv Malhotra who himself had such a heightened and profound level of spirituality which helped me view yoga in a new light. But what is more important is to realise the value of yoga in helping you make peace with what you look like, what you believe in, who you are as an individual, and expressing yourself freely. All this might seem a useless mumbo-jumbo right now. But trust me, here and now is when you can lay the foundation of a solid and substantial personality, which will make you grow from strength to still more strength.

So here is what we are going to do. Let us start with giving you a **Basic Yoga Routine** that you must follow at least four times a week for an hour each day. This will not only help you deal with the physical imbalances, but will also ensure a calm and uncluttered thought process.

Step 1

Sit in any comfortable position, and begin with **deep and gentle breathing**. There are three things you need to keep in mind while doing so —

1. Make sure as you 'inhale', you expand the chest and stomach out, and when you 'exhale', you contract the chest and stomach in.

2. Make sure your spine is absolutely straight and you do not move your shoulders while breathing. Normally, when someone asks us to breathe deep, we tend to move our shoulders up and down. However, the correct way is actually to lay greater emphasis on the movement of your chest and stomach forward and backward.

3. Be conscious of hearing the sound of your breathing through your nasal passage, slowly and steadily increasing the ratio of inhaling and exhaling. This means that the amount of time you take to breathe

in should gradually be doubled while breathing out. Let your breathing flow *rhythmically*, be at ease and try to enjoy the process. That is the only way to make your senses and system respond positively.

Step 2

Lie down straight on the ground. Make sure you have a thin yoga mat underneath. Leave the body totally relaxed and free of any tension. Breathe in deep once more as you stretch your hands up, opening up all your joints, muscles and ligaments.

While breathing out, bring your hands down by the side of the body, and get ready for a little warming-up session before the *asanas*. Now there are three basic warm-up steps. You can follow any one at a time, but make sure you alternate between them.

1. Join your legs together, stretch your toes, keep your knees straight and rotate legs clockwise in a big circle, inhaling as you take your legs up, and exhaling as you begin to bring them down. Repeat this three times. Take a break and then repeat the same movement anti-clockwise three times. Just make sure you do this really slowly and gently, without any jerks or sudden movements to the back.

2. Try forward cycling motion in the air with the legs. The breathing process must continue along with the movement. Repeat this process three times.

3. As you inhale, pull your legs and hands towards each other, compressing the stomach muscles, and raising your upper back and neck too. As you exhale, straighten out the legs, hands and back. Repeat it three times.

All these little warm-ups are essential to initiate movement in your spine, stomach and limbs to release any stiffness or stress.

Step 3: Asana 1

Sarvang Asana
(90° Asana)

The first *asana* that lays the foundation is this one. Its actual name is **Sarvang Asana**. I prefer referring to the *asanas* by names that we can associate with easily in our daily use lingo. It is not the name that matters, it is the precision and grace while performing it that actually helps you derive the real benefit.

• Stay in the lying position. All you need to do is to start by raising one leg, straight and stretched out up to 90° (inhale as you do so), hold the position up to a count of 10 and do keep breathing simultaneously. Then as slowly and gently as you can, start lowering the leg down (exhale as you do so) and get it back to the ground. Repeat the same with the other leg with the same sequence of breathing. And finally, raise both the legs together.

Benefits: This *asana* is for the base of your spine. Remember, this is the place where the *muladhara chakra* is located! It also helps in strengthening the stomach muscles, thereby improving your digestion.

Step 4: Asana 2

Mayur Asana

(Back Raise Asana)

Turn around and lie down on your stomach. Place your hands by the side of your body and get ready for ***Mayur Asana***.

• Form a fist position of your hands, place your chin and shoulders on the ground, focus your eyes on any one point in the front, and slowly raise one leg up, without bending your knee (inhale as you do so). Hold the leg up to a count of 10 (continue breathing), and gently begin lowering your leg down (as you exhale). Repeat the same action with the other leg and finally raise both the legs up, absolutely straight and stretched out.

Benefits: It benefits the lower abdomen region, where the *svadhisthana chakra* is located. It also strengthens the spine.

Step 5: Asana 3

Vakra Asana

(Crocodile Asana)

- Relax in the *Vakra Asana*. Keep lying on your stomach with feet in opposite directions, that is, heels in and toes out with legs at a distance and hands under your forehead. You can turn your neck on your side and totally relax your shoulders, spine and legs.

Benefits: The main benefit of this *asana* is to give your body a little time to absorb the movements of the previous *asanas*. It also makes sure that there is no undue stress building up anywhere along the spine, diverting the tension in opposite direction.

Step 6: Asana 4

Bhujanga Asana

(Up-stretch Asana)

While lying down on the stomach, get ready for the *Bhujanga Asana*.

- Place your hands under your shoulders with legs and feet straight. Gradually start to raise your chin, chest, upper abdomen, middle and lower abdomen, taking full support of your hands, wrists and elbows (inhale as you raise yourself). Make sure the pelvic region is in touch with the ground.

- Bring the stretch right up to your throat and neck focusing your eyes at a point on the ceiling. Hold the position (continue breathing) and then slowly start bending your elbows, bringing down your lower abdomen, middle and upper abdomen, chest, chin and forehead on the ground (exhale in this sequence).

Benefits: Essential benefits are for the upper abdomen area, where the *manipura chakra* is located, and also for enhancing the flexibility of the spine and releasing stress from neck and shoulder zone.

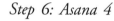

Step 7: Asana 5

Baal Asana

(Infant Pose)

Relax in *Baal Asana*.

- Keep lying on your stomach and turn your neck to your side. Bend the leg and arm of the same side just enough to help you relax and leave the other side loose. Repeat the same position on the other side.

Benefits: It mainly helps you ease out the neck and shoulder zone to avoid any chance of building up of tension at any point. It also leaves the body free and fluid as that of a child.

Step 8: Asana 6

Dhanur Asana

(Arch-shape Asana)

While still lying on the stomach, get ready for the *Dhanur Asana*.

- Fold your legs and try holding your ankles with your hands. Press the heels to your hip joint, then steadily raise your chin and chest up (as you inhale) while you stabilise this pose. Slowly try to raise your knees slightly above the ground (keep breathing as you hold this pose).

- Balance only on your entire abdominal region, hold till a count of ten then slowly first bring your knees down and then your chest and chin (as you exhale). Release the grip of your hands around the ankles, and lie down straight, relaxing once again in *Baal asana*.

Benefits: The main benefit of this *asana* is to stimulate your entire digestive system and the arch backwards. It further enhances flexibility and strength of the spinal cord.

Step 9: Asana 7

Sukht Pawan Mukt Asana

(Compression Asana)

Turn around on your back, lie down straight, and get ready for the *Sukht Pawan Mukt Asana*.

- All you need to do is bend your legs and raise them towards your stomach, wrapping your arms around your legs. Tightening the grip slowly raise your neck up and try to get your chin in contact with the knees (inhale as you form the compression).

- Hold the pose for a count of ten but do not hold the breathing. While releasing the *asana*, first lower your neck slowly, then loosen up the hands, and then release the legs (all this while exhaling).

Benefits: The main advantage is to flush out all the toxins, impurities and blockages from your chest and abdomen through the compression. At the same time, it releases the back of any tension knots and strain.

After this, turn on any one side and get up on the side of your body but not up straight because that is what puts excessive pressure on the spine. Sit straight, getting geared up with the sitting down asanas.

Did you think this was the end? Well, not so soon!

Step 10: Asana 8

Ardha Matsyendra Asana

(Towel Twisting Asana)

We start the sitting *asanas* with the all-in-one *Ardha Matsyendra Asana.*

- Place one foot at the base of your thigh; take the other leg across and place the foot of that leg next to the knee of the first leg which is on the upper side.

- Place the hand on the same side on ground towards the spine, while twisting around the other hand towards the thigh of the leg which is on the upper side. Keep breathing steadily. Just remember, the more you place the hand on the ground towards the spine, greater would be the twist to the spine, and the more you extend the front hand towards the thigh, the greater will be the twist to your stomach and chest.

- To give the final twist to your neck and throat, turn your head in the extreme opposite direction, keeping your eyes focused on the line of your shoulder. While returning back, remember to breathe out. First of all, get your neck straight, then the upper arm and then the upper leg. Repeat this sequence with the other side too. That sure sounds complicated. In fact, I myself feel breathless with that description! But once you practise it a couple of times and observe the picture carefully, it would not seem so arduous.

- Before we move on to the next *asana*, I am sure you would like to know why I called it the 'towel twisting asana'. As you twist a wet towel from one end to another to drain out all the excess water, similarly in this pose, we simply induce a twist in the body right from the legs to the entire spine, stomach, chest, up to the neck and throat. This helps to drain out all the excess stiffness, undigested toxins, impurities and blockages from one end to another, leaving you light and floating.

Benefits: The *asana* is useful in cleansing the entire system and in turn purifying blood circulation by massaging your heart, which is where your fourth *chakra*, the *anahata*, is located. Most of all, it releases undue stress and rigidity from the spine.

Step 11

Sit back and relax a bit. Give your body time to regain its normal bio-rhythm. Stretch out and proceed.

Step 12: Asana 9

Paschimottan Asana

(Sandwich Press Asana)

In this *asana* you sit and extend both legs forward, parallel to and touching each other. Extend both arms straight on top (inhale as you rise) and gently bring the arms down, forward (as you exhale), holding the toes with your fingers.

- Try to bring your forehead as much in contact with the knees as possible and hold this position till a count of ten (keep breathing simultaneously). While returning, first raise your face and neck up, then stretch your hands up, straightening up your spine (inhale as you come up).

Benefits: The main benefits lie in its two-way action. It squeezes the abdomen and gives compression to the digestive tract. Also it brings the maximum elongation for the spine, making both the stomach and the spine less rigid and more flexible.

Step 13: Asana 10

Vajra Asana

(Namaaz Asana)

The *Vajra Asana* essentially involves sitting with your legs folded under your hip joint with a continuous flow of breathing accompanying the position.

- For increasing focus and concentration skills, it is advisable to sit in this *asana* and further modify it to the ***Shashank Asana (Analysis Pose)*** by simply continuing to sit in *Vajra Asana* and bending forward (while exhaling) to place your elbow joints together on the ground, placing your chin in the palms in front and gazing into the empty space, just analysing the events of your day, the good, the bad, actions, reactions, and ways of making your interaction in every sphere more purpose-oriented. It really helps clear the clutter and chaos that clouds the mind.

Benefits: The main benefit derived from this particular *asana* is that since the entire weight of your body is lying on the soles of your feet, it initiates fast digestion by applying pressure at that part of your feet where the roots of your stomach, intestines, colon, etc. are located.

Step 14

Relax in the same position in *Vajra Asana* by simply leaving your hands loose and placing your forehead on the ground. While bending forward, normal breathing must continue all throughout, and when you feel like coming up, first of all raise your face and neck and thereafter straighten up your spine (do this while inhaling simultaneously). This position relieves you of all your mental stress and unnecessary thinking, and instils the most positive thoughts and energies in you.

After touching upon these basic sitting asanas, it is time we stride forward to our next destination, that is, the 'standing asanas'. So simply stand up on your knees and raise your hands forward. Now first balance yourself on one foot and then on the other, standing up straight. Be careful even while making these small insignificant transitional moves from lying to sitting to standing. Make sure that the gestures of your body remain gentle and gradual. Avoid any unnecessary jerks to the joints and spine. Even though you are young and kicking, it is the foundation that you lay today that will make or break your system 5, 10 or 15 years from now. Long-term planning is what is cooler — so trust me and play along.

Step15: Asana 11

Trikona Asana

(Triangle Asana)

Trikona Asana derives its name simply from the shape that the body forms. You start by keeping your legs at a distance, at least a foot and a half apart and placing your hands in a straight line at shoulder level with the palms facing in front. The direction of one foot should be at right angle while the other should face sideways.

- Inhale and slowly bend (while exhaling) on the side of your torso towards the foot facing sideways. Try to maintain the bend only on the side with maximum stretching of your waist. Make sure you are neither falling backwards nor forwards (continue breathing as long as you hold up to a count of 10).

- Then slowly and gently start straightening up sideways (while inhaling).

- Take a tiny-winy break and repeat the same on the other side in precisely similar sequence.

Benefits: The main benefit of this movement is that it laterally induces stimulation in the liver and also strengthens the spine, in addition to toning up the waist.

One cardinal point you must keep in mind while performing the standing set of asanas is that, they focus more on the 'mudra' aspect wherein the grace quotient has to be at its peak. So be very aware of your gestures and rhythm while performing them.

Step 16: Asana 12

Tada Asana

(Mountain Pose)

Tada Asana is my personal favourite because not only does it make you physically stronger, but also boosts your will-power. As the name suggests, this *asana* makes the system as strong and stable as the mountains.

- Stand straight with legs at a distance in proportion with your body frame. Now start raising only the soles of your feet slowly, somewhat like a ballet dancer, with maximum weight on the tips of your toes (inhale as you do so) and if the balance can be maintained then also slowly raise your hands straight up getting a full stretch (this too while inhaling).

- The trick is to keep your mind focused on the sound of your breathing and your eyes on a single point in front to slowly fade out all other thoughts, sounds and visions, focusing thereby, purely on your own space. This is where the will-power and your ability to use the mind come in. You, therefore, become the person in-charge of yourself.

Benefits: The stretching action from toes to fingertips with active breathing allows you to absorb abundance of fresh oxygenated air into the opened up system. It also helps you derive lots of positive energy from the surroundings and overall toning of the entire body.

> *Relax a bit. Do a little loose twisting of the torso and arms side to side, calm down totally and then move on to the next asana.*

Step 17: Asana 13

Katimanthana Asana

(Twisting Tango Asana)

- In this *asana*, you simply stand straight. Place the feet at a distance (half a foot apart), extend the arms horizontally at shoulder level and fixing the feet nice and firm. Only twist the torso and arms, first in one extreme direction, with eyes focused on the farthest point in the opposite direction (while inhaling) then return to the front (while exhaling), and repeat the same action on the other side. Make sure your knees don't bend as you twist.

Benefits: This swinging twist keeps the spine free of tension, knots or any stiffness, and allows fluid and free movement to the body, preventing it from becoming rigid, especially the neck and upper back zone.

> *After this exhaustive series of asanas, which should be a regular routine for each one of you blooming buds, let us not forget the oh-so-important 'breath of fresh air' on which you shall thrive. So coming up is the process of 'pranayama' that needs to be a regular feature of your routine.*

Step 18: Pranayama

1. Anulom-Vilom

(Alternate Breathing)

The very first aspect of the *pranayama* features ***Anulom-Vilom*** in which all you need to understand is the role of both your nasal passages. While the right nostril carries greater proportions of 'heat energy', the left carries greater 'cooling energy'. The former is *pingala* and the latter is *ida* in technical yogic terms. So all we are trying here is to strike the perfect balance between the proportions of heat and cold energies (*sushumna*) that are flowing through your lungs.

- You begin by first checking which of the two nasal passages is relatively more open. Then take the *mudra* of your hand in a manner where the first two fingers are held firmly under the thumb. Then simply close the blocked passage with your thumb and inhale gently but long and deep through the open one. Slowly release through the alternate, blocked passage and without taking a break, continue to inhale from the blocked nasal passage and release from the open passage which you began with.

- This completes one full cycle, and should ideally be repeated at least 4-5 times. Make sure that in the process, your spine should be absolutely straight, the elbows at right angles, not slouching down.

- And, it is equally essential to ensure that the amount of time you take to inhale is doubled while exhaling. I also advise you to keep your eyes closed to derive the maximum pleasure of absorbing this fresh, pure, oxygenated air to every nook and corner of your lungs. This also keeps your sixth chakra, the *aina chakra*, completely enlightened.

2. Vissudha Pranayama

(Snoring Sound Breathing)

The second aspect of your basic *pranayama* routine deals with cleansing your throat passage by means of *Vissudha Pranayama,* which I am sure most of you do not even consider as part of the breathing passage. Remember all those nasty throat allergies, coughs and septic pains. Well, here is the remedy which actually works! It is also effective for the thyroid gland.

- You basically need to let the air pass through the throat, touching its surface and gently. You should even release it through the throat itself. In the beginning, it might sound like an obnoxious snoring sound, but with practice, it will become smoother.

- Eventually, it creates a cooling sensation penetrating deep down till your lungs. It greatly helps in enlightening the fifth chakra — the *vissudha chakra.* Repeat this *pranayama* 4-5 times patiently.

3. Bhramari Pranayama

(Mental Vibration)

The third basic level of the *pranayama* includes the *Bhramari Pranayama* wherein you sit straight, close your ears with your thumbs and place fingers on the eyes to keep them closed.

- All that you have to keep open and receptive is your mind, while you take out a humming voice from your throat centre without opening your mouth. Slowly keep breathing in, and while exhaling, take out this vibration from the throat simultaneously.

- Let it travel and resonate through your system right up to your *sahasrara chakra,* massaging each and every nerve in the brain and draining all your tensions and stress with every vibration that travels from the mouth till your brain. Suddenly when you open your eyes and ears, it is like a calm descending upon your otherwise over-pressurised senses. On the whole, it helps you clear up the clutter and chaos from your mind.

Step 19: Asana 14

Padma Asana

Lotus Pose and Om Chanting

As we are inching towards the end, let us top up your schedule with cooling down procedures. These procedures on one hand calm the body down, and on the other hand make sure that it seals all the absorbed energy. This includes sitting in the *Padma Asana*. It is one of the best remedies for indigestion, and correcting spine and leg nerve rigidity. This *asana* should also be followed by *Om* chanting, which is imperative during meditation.

• Sit with crossing one foot on the opposite thigh and the other foot placed on the other thigh. If you cannot manage both, then even one foot would do. Slowly take a deep breath and say **OOAAAAMMMMMM**. It looks funny as you read, but you will understand the real flow and feel only by this description. See, the word '*Om*' is made up of three alphabets 'o', 'a' and 'm'. Each alphabet produces certain amount of energies, which help you connect with the positive vibes in and around you. So even though you say the word in one flow in your mind, the amount of time you take while speaking 'o' doubles while you speak 'a' and becomes the longest while you speak 'm'.

• *Om* possesses the innate ability of piercing through all the layers reaching your core, your true self, thereby helping you reconnect with your soul. So repeat it as many times as you like with faith, belief and conviction. You will literally feel as if you have reached a floating, weightless state of existence. I am sure you would not mind reaching cloud nine.

Step 20: Asana 15

Surya Namaskar

(Sun Salutation)

Surya Namaskar encompasses almost each and every *asana* and *mudra* in its very basic form combined with the coordination of breathing. I love calling it the 'Sun Salutation'. The essence of performing this twelve-step-continuum is to absorb the maximum energy from the ultimate source of light and energy that sustains all life on Earth — the SUN. This process is simply a means of paying your adulation and respect to the Sun. So while performing this *asana*, your mind must be calm, your body receptive and your soul like an empty vessel, ready to absorb all that is positive, good and healthy.

1. *The Namaskar* — Stretch out your hands on the sides as you inhale. Raise hands on top joining them, and as you exhale, gently place them in the centre of your chest, near the *anahata chakra*.

2. *Parvat Asana (The Arch)* — Raise hands in a joint position as you inhale, and while exhaling, bend backwards, only the torso and arms, bringing a slight arch in the upper back.

3. *Hasta Pada Asana (The Compression)* — Inhale, straighten up your arms gently while exhaling. Place hands behind the legs and bring your forehead as much in contact with the knees as you can. Continue breathing.

4. *Ek Pada Prasaran (The One Foot Balance)* — Place both your hands on the ground at shoulder distance apart. While exhaling, stretch one leg behind as much as you can and balance up on your fingertips. Inhale as you give a little arch to your neck upwards and join your hands.

5. *Bhoodhar Asana* — Bring the hands fully in contact with the ground. Look in front and as you inhale, stretch the second leg behind at the same level as the first. The main fulcrum of this pose comes at the base of your spine. It is like a triangle with hip joint forming the peak, and arms and legs providing support. Make sure you keep the heels of your foot pressed to the ground and continue breathing.

6. *Ashtanga Pranipat Asana (The Flat Out)* — While exhaling, bend your elbows, knees and lie flat in contact with the ground. Make sure you do not change the position of your hands and place your forehead on the ground. Place your feet flat too, fully relaxed.

7. *Bhujanga Asana (Up-stretch Asana)* — With the support of hands, wrists and elbows, gently raise your chin, chest and upper-middle-lower abdomen as you inhale. Keep breathing as you hold the stretch. While lowering yourself down, follow the same sequence.

8. *Back in Bhoodhar Asana* — As you lie flat, slowly take support of your hands under the shoulder to raise your upper body and take support of your feet, toes, knees to raise your lower body. This triangular position lends maximum enlightenment to the base of your spine, the *muladhara chakra.*

9. *Ek Pada Prasaran (Back in One Foot Balance)* — Same as before, but this time get the second foot in front.

10. *Hasta Pada Asana (Back in Compression)* — Inhale and get the second foot up in standing position, but your back should remain bent forward with the hands once again behind your legs and forehead to the knee.

11. *Parvat Asana (Back in Arch)* — As you inhale, stretch your hands slowly and gradually straighten up. Make sure that your face straightens up first, followed by your neck and then your back. Exhale and bend backwards.

12. *Daksh Asana (Finally Wrap-up Namaskar)* — Simply inhale while straightening out. Join your hands, and while exhaling, bring the hands back from where you started, that is, in the centre of your chest, near *anahata chakra*.

It is pretty simple if you realise that it is the same sequence that is being repeated in the beginning as well as in the end. There are only two steps of *bhujanga* and *ashtanga pranipat asanas* that are set apart.

At the end of this 'twenty-point-programme', there are a few general pointers that you must keep in mind at all times while following this routine.

- Try performing this schedule first thing in the morning after having a glass of water and a visit to the loo. If it is too cumbersome to get up early then take care that while performing it during the day, you must have a gap of approximately 2-3 hours after a meal.

- Never ever push your body movements beyond your comfort level. Be very aware of this because the aim of yoga should be to work *with* your body and not *against* it.

- Be aware not to ever hold your breath while in an *asana*. The only coordination you need to maintain is the one between your movements and inhaling or exhaling. As a general rule, always synchronise an upward movement with inhaling and a downward movement with exhaling.

- While holding the *asana*, the count that I have referred to can be modified depending on how long you feel comfortable in that posture. Just remember, the count that you give yourself should be reasonable and not a rattling one because the only person you will be duping is you. So be honest!

- Correlating the *asanas*, *mudras* and *pranayama* methods with the location of *chakras* and the specific physical, mental, spiritual, emotional issues that they deal with, will only help you further clarify the significance and benefits of performing them.

- The number of times you wish to repeat a certain *asana* or breathing process depends entirely upon your comfort zone and how effective you wish to make the routine.

I have left pretty much everything to your better judgement, because I truly believe that I can only show you the 'how' and more importantly the 'why' of yoga, the 'when' and 'where' are totally your choices. Just make sure whenever you choose to get on to this routine or if you are already following it, it must be fuelled by an enthusiasm and strong sense of belief in its benefits.

Last but definitely not the least is the *remedy* for those of you battling with the following issues:

- If you have **disturbed menstrual cycles**, then try to avoid *asanas* that involve inversions and exert pressure on your lower abdomen in the first two days of your periods. To ease out the pain, I prescribe following a regular routine of *pranayama, vajra asana, sukht pawan mukt asana* and *tada asana*. It will keep your breathing smooth, your digestion activated and spine stress-free. Drink at least 6-8 glasses of water (lukewarm in case of pain). Have lots of green vegetables, salads and fresh fruits.

- Those of you **hassled by weight** must follow the mentioned routine religiously and special emphasis must be on performing *pranayama* for longer periods and *surya namaskar* at least 3-4 times. Increase the intake of water to 8-10 glasses. Start your day with lukewarm glass of water with a squeeze of lime (if you are not too prone to acidity). Sip on it and see the kick-start it gives you.

- Coming on to **the pimples and acne**, all you need to do is to keep your breathing passage totally free from blockages. Again, drink lots of water. Make it a habit to even travel with a bottle wherever you go. Be sure to increase the intake of fruits in your diet, because what you eat is what shows on your skin.

- **Height** is an issue that I am sure you have been nagged with a hundred times, but don't you fret. We have a solution. All you need to do is focus on the standing *asanas*, like *tada asana*, because they stretch all the ligaments, joints and muscles, thereby giving you that toned-up look.

- Finally the **'ace grades' pressure** by parents and teachers. Tackle this with special emphasis on the *pranayama* procedure, especially *bhramari* and *Om chanting* which tend to relax the mind, drain of unnecessary tensions and help you retain all the meaningful information. *Anulom-vilom* greatly helps in enhancing concentration and focus.

On the whole, just remember to respect your body. Learn its language so that you can provide it with all the ingredients that will make it respond to your needs more actively. Keep your senses alive, open and receptive at all times. These are the doors and windows that filter all your thoughts, feelings and determine your actions. To put it in simpler terms, learn to value the present moment and have fun in every situation. Everything is an opportunity, if taken rightly.

The Transitional Twenties

It is ironic how most of us in our twenties feel like we have arrived at a pretty much 'sorted out', 'been there' and 'done that' kind of a stage in life. Having completed graduation and moving on to choosing professional courses, little do we realise that the ordeal has just begun. From peer-pressure to carving out a profession-pressure, to parental pressure, you get the dose all in one go. Not to miss those of us who also get bombed with the 'boyfriend' blunder! I swear by first hand experience, it can be quite a transition.

So you are left wondering where a discipline as serene and spiritual as yoga fits into this chaos. For one, it simply acts like a little getaway from all the hassles, hectic routines, analysis, expectations and judgements that one gets flooded with. And while you are on this trip, the real sorting of issues begins. Even though some of you might already be practising yoga as a remedy of physical disorders and imbalances, you tend to disregard the fact that each of your disorders or imbalances manifests from a deep-rooted mental and emotional offset. This counterbalance sets in at this transitional shift where you are no longer treated as a kid and neither are you given the privilege of a full-fledged adult.

Having gone through these dilemmas myself, I would like to share with you some remedies that I found solace in. I hope they work their wonder on you too. All you need is a strong sense of commitment to yourself and that is not too hard to make, if you love and respect yourself. If you are in a prior habit of doing yoga and know how these moves work, then I am sure this schedule will help you take the leap from the realm that you might be restricting yourself to.

Step 1

The first thing you need to ensure is to disengage yourself from the routine events of the day. Fade out all your interactions whether good and bad as well as people's actions and reactions. Constantly remind yourself that this time that you have chosen to dedicate to yourself is meant purely to create a space. This is the space where you can rejuvenate, relax and replenish all your energies and emotions that get drained into the rut of mechanical routines.

i. Sit in any comfortable position in a fresh, open space and begin with deep and gentle breathing. There are three things you need to keep in mind while doing so.

  • Make sure as you 'inhale', you expand the chest and stomach out, but when you 'exhale', you 'contract' the chest and stomach in.

  • Make sure your spine is absolutely straight and you do not move your shoulders while breathing. Normally when someone asks us to breathe deep, we tend to move our shoulders up and down. However, the correct way is actually to lay greater emphasis on the movement of your chest and stomach forward and backward.

  • Be conscious of hearing the sound of your breathing through your nasal passage, slowly and steadily increasing the ratio of inhaling and exhaling. That means that the amount of time you take to breathe in should gradually be doubled while breathing out.

All technicalities aside, just let your breathing flow rhythmically; be at ease and try to enjoy the process. That is the only way to make your senses and system respond positively. Even if you have been practising this process before, try to bring the three aspects mentioned above in-synch. Only then you can expect a thorough cleansing to occur.

ii. ***Warm-up:*** After relieving your system of all its pollutants and impurities, it is now time to synthesise the mind with the body. Lie down straight on the ground onto a thin yoga mat. Leave the body relaxed and free of any tension. Breathe in deep once more as you stretch your hands up, opening up all your joints, muscles and ligaments. While breathing out, bring your hands down by the side of the body, and get ready for a little warming-up session before the *asanas*. There are three basic warm-up steps. You can follow any one at a time, but make sure you alternate between them.

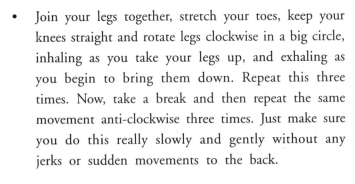

• Join your legs together, stretch your toes, keep your knees straight and rotate legs clockwise in a big circle, inhaling as you take your legs up, and exhaling as you begin to bring them down. Repeat this three times. Now, take a break and then repeat the same movement anti-clockwise three times. Just make sure you do this really slowly and gently without any jerks or sudden movements to the back.

• Put your legs together without bending your knees. Keep your toes stretched out and raise your legs just up to a 30° elevation. Inhale as you do so. Hold the position up to a count of 15. Keep a steady rate of breathing at this point while releasing the legs down. Be as slow and stable as you can while exhaling simultaneously. This movement strengthens the stomach muscles as well as makes the leg muscles and nerves stronger.

- As you inhale, pull your legs and hands towards each other, compressing the stomach muscles and raising your upper back and neck too. As you exhale, straighten out the legs, hands and back. Repeat three times.

All these little warm-ups are essential to initiate movement in your spine, stomach and limbs to release any stiffness or stress. Now, slowly lie down straight.

Step 2: Asana 1

Sarvang Asana

(90° Asana)

As you already know, this *asana* lays the foundation. You may refer to this *asana* in 'The Troublesome Teenage' on pages 28-29.

Step 3: Asana 2

Salamba Sarvang Asana

(Elbow Stand Asana)

Taking the same movement of **Sarvang Asana**, we move a step forward into the **Salamba Sarvang Asana**. All you need to focus on is the gap that you are able to create between the hip joint and the ground level. This is directly correlated to the degree of the flexibility of your spine, as well as strength that you possess in your wrists, elbows and shoulders.

- Raise your legs straight up to 90°, gently and gracefully, without any jerks or hasty movements as you inhale. Then take the support of your palms and elbows to push the weight of your body upwards.

Gently place the hands at the base of your spine, more towards the hip joint. Straighten out the hips and the legs, with your feet stretched out as you keep inhaling, balancing the entire weight on the elbows, shoulders and hands to prevent undue stress on the neck.

• Try to maintain the body weight in a forward direction. Avoid falling backwards. Hold the position till a count of 15 and keep breathing simultaneously. This position enlightens not only the *muladhara*, but also the *svadisthana* and *manipura chakras*. Therefore it is very beneficial for the liver, heart and thyroid gland.

• While returning too, slowly place the hands one by one on the ground, taking their full support without giving a single jerk to the spine. Come back to the 90° and steadily start lowering the legs back to normal at a snail speed while exhaling.

• Constantly focus your eyes on the toes and your mind on the sound of your breathing, without letting it wander to random thoughts, like which movie you have to catch or which friends you would go out for a party with or the fight you had with mom etc etc. Cut it all out and learn to use your will-power. Condition the mind and body instead of being used by them. This single-minded dedication is what brings out the real flavour and essence of your movements.

• Be sure to relax, giving the body a little time to absorb the benefits of this *asana* which revolve around enhancing your spine strength, stretching your ligaments through the neck, spine, hip joint, leg nerves right down till the tips of your toes. In addition, it is the best remedy to release any uneasy indigestion sensation. Trust me once the digestion compartment is taken care of, it is like sorting out Pandora's Box of illnesses and diseases.

Step 4: Asana 3

Neeralam Asana

(Neck Strain Drain Asana)

Slowly turn around and lie down on your stomach. Stretch out your hands and feet bringing the entire length and breadth of your body in contact with the ground. At this point, once again clear up the clutter in your mind. Reconnect with energies flowing in and around you.

- Begin with setting your legs at a distance, placing your feet in opposite directions (heels in and toes out). Slowly place both your elbows on the ground together raising your chin and chest up to your upper abdomen with your chin held by your palms. Join your hands, place your thumbs under the tip of your chin and give it the best stretch upwards that you can manage. Inhale as you do so.

- Focus your eyes on a single point on the ceiling — this in turn releases all the pressure, stiffness from the sensitive neck area, and stretches the throat enlightening your *vissudha chakra*.

- Gradually place the chin back on the palms. Gently as you inhale, twist only the neck portion. Now keeping your hands, arms and legs fixed, try to get a side vision of your feet or legs. Hold the position while you continue to breathe till a patient count of 15. Slowly, without any sudden movements of the neck, exhale and return to the original position. Repeat the same twist on the other side as well.

- After completing the process, give one final stretch to the neck upwards with your thumbs and then gently while exhaling, lower your elbows, place your hands under your forehead, and turn your head on any one side. Keep your feet in opposite directions and relax in the *Vakra Asana*.

Benefits: The main benefits that ensue from this asana are to help drain and release any stress that tends to build around the neck and shoulder area in the due course of the day. So even if you are aware of the nitty-gritty of it all, it is the applicability at the right time and right place that makes these tools worth it.

Step 5: Asana 4

Bhujanga Asana

(Up-stretch Asana)

To further enhance the curvature in the neck and stretch in the throat while lying down on the stomach, *Bhujanga Asana* is very beneficial. If you are looking at toning up of your abdomen muscles, this position is extremely beneficial. Furthermore, there is a feeling of relief that descends over you, as if someone has just lifted the entire burden off your shoulders.

Believing in these mental constructs greatly enriches your receptivity. So do not restrict the gains till the physical, and do leave enough room to let them seep to your core.

Please refer to this *asana* in 'The Troublesome Teenage' on page 30.

Step 6: Asana 5

Shalabh Asana

(See-saw Pose)

After relaxing in *Vakra Asana* for a split second, let us make way for **Shalabh Asana**. This, in a way, is the opposite of *Bhujanga Asana* since here the emphasis is on raising the lower part of the body as opposed to the upper.

- All one needs to remember is to begin with placing both the hands in fist position over the base of the spine, and gently as you inhale, raise both your legs up absolutely straight, only up to a level where your knees do not bend and the upper part of the body (chin and shoulders) remain fixed on the ground, while elbows are in the air.

- Continue breathing as you hold this pose till a standard count of 15, then while exhaling, patiently lower the legs down, relaxing the hands as well. The main impact comes to your lower abdomen region, where the *svadisthana* is located. As you breathe and balance at this point, it massages all your organs, replenishing them.

Benefits: The essential benefits are directed towards the leg nerves and muscles. Holding all these positions has a direct impact on building the power of your mind, body and soul.

Step 7: Asana 6

Dhanur Asana

(Arch-shape Asana)

While still lying on the stomach, get ready for *Dhanur Asana.* Fold your legs and try holding your ankles with your hands, pressing the heels to your hip joint, and then steadily raising your chin and chest up as you inhale. Raise your knees also, then gently fall on one side stretch and then fall on second side stretch. Please refer to this *asana* in 'The Troublesome Teenage' on page 31.

Relax in Baal Asana (Infant Pose)

This *asana* is the same as given in 'The Troublesome Teenage' on page 31. The aim of this *asana* is to induce a child-like fluidity in your movements and gestures, just to remind you of those childhood days when life was simple, uncluttered and you floated effortlessly with the tide of life. As we grow up, certain rigidity creeps into our system and senses. Since you are at the threshold, now is the time to reset the rhythm to its original tune.

So what are you waiting for? Go ahead and set yourself free.

Step 8: Asana 7

Sukht Pawan Mukt Asana

(Compression Asana)

This *asana* can be referred to in 'The Troublesome Teenage' on page 32. The main advantage of this *asana* is to flush out all the toxins, impurities and blockages from your chest and abdomen through the compression. At the same time, it releases the back of any tension knots or strain. It thus has an all-encompassing impact on the three *chakras*, that is, the *svadisthana* in the lower abdomen, *manipura* in the upper abdomen and the *anahata* in the centre of your chest.

- Slowly turn on one side, as you release the neck but keep the grip around legs; repeat the turn on second side.

- Make sure you relax taking this foetal position once again, just roll on your back, up and down in a pendulum motion, to release any last bits of tension along the spinal cord. As you relax, become aware of the upsurging energy through the spinal channel, resonating and spreading to every nook and corner of your system and senses.

Once you are done up to this point, it is essential to become aware of how the lying down asanas have a greater bearing, on the enhancement of the flexibility of your spine, and holistic energy activation, through this vital lifeline channel. However as you make your way to the next stage of 'sitting asanas', you will instinctively realise how these set of asanas give a boost to your entire digestive tract, encompassing all your stomach organs and intestinal pathway.

Step 9: Asana 8

Ardha Matsyendra Asana

(Towel Twisting Asana)

Please refer to this *asana* in 'The Troublesome Teenage' on page 33.

Take a break because you would surely need to relax after all that twisting around. Just remember never push yourself beyond your comfort level. If, at any point, you feel a strain, just ease out the pose, stretch out and then try again. Also if you are trying these *asanas* for the very first time, or after a long break, or you are at the beginner's level, be sure to proceed step by step. It might take you months before you can acquire the final pose perfectly.

Step 10: Asana 9

Paschimottan Asana

(Sandwich Press Asana)

This *asana* can be referred to in 'The Troublesome Teenage' on page 34. It makes both the stomach and the spine more flexible. So it is like squeezing a sponge, making sure it remains soft and supple.

Step 11: Asana 10

Vajra Asana

(Namaaz Asana)

Please refer to this *asana* in 'The Troublesome Teenage' on page 35.

Have you ever wondered why Muslims sit the way they do while performing their prayers? Well, that is because it is one of the best ways to 'cleanse and purify' your system and release all the negative energy that clogs the circulation. This in turn creates the ideal state of mind to meditate and pray in.

The main benefit derived from this particular *asana* comes from the principle that since the entire weight of your body is lying on the soles of your feet, it initiates fast digestion by applying pressure at that part of your feet where the roots of your stomach, intestines, colon etc are located.

Step 12: Asana 11

Shashank Asana

(Analysis Pose)

Further modify it to **Shashank Asana** by simply continuing to sit in *Vajra Asana* and bending forward (while exhaling) to place your elbows together on the ground, placing your chin in the palms in front and gazing into the empty space just analysing the events of your day, the good, the bad, actions, reactions, and ways of making your interaction in every sphere more purpose-oriented. It is greatly beneficial to enhance your focus and concentration skills.

- Relax in the same position in *Vajra Asana*, by simply leaving your hands loose and placing your forehead on the ground. While bending forward, normal breathing must continue all throughout. When you feel like coming up, raise your face and neck, and thereafter straighten up your spine (do these while inhaling simultaneously). This position ensures that you decompress all the mental stress, unnecessary thinking, and retain only the most positive thoughts and energies with you.

Reaching the final round of this marathon, let us discuss the 'standing asanas'. One aspect that you need to focus on at all times while performing these set of asanas is that herein lies the ultimate test of your ability to fade out all distractions and routine thoughts. It makes you engage purely in an internal dialogue, making an honest connection with your true self. Now if you have already been practising all these asanas before and have never thought about viewing them in this light, all I can say is that it is never too late to make amends.

Let me put it this way — all of us as social beings thoroughly relish interacting with our relatives, friends, family, and even complete strangers, making the effort to gel with them, feel pleasant and make great conversations. Ironically, when it boils down to spending some quiet and isolated moments, connecting us with our own personal thoughts, feelings and working towards refining and balancing them out, then it seems to be such an ordeal. That is because through our growing-up years, we all have been conditioned to operate only at a surface, the face value level in the way we present ourselves, our mannerisms, etiquettes etc. Little do we realise that we have slowly lost on making the most essential relationship and that is with the 'person' sitting deep inside each one of us.

The way you treat this insider is what shall reflect in the way you wish to interact with the world at large. So please, each time you perform these asanas, put your soul into them. Their steps, sequences and technicalities are all secondary. The real message is the art you have to master. So let us get started!

Step 13: Asana 12

Tada Asana

(Mountain Pose)

It is my personal favourite, since there is very little technicality involved and its gesture make me feel like the one who is trying to reach out to the skies.

This *asana* enhances your will-power and your ability to use the mind. Let this be a key to unlock your mind room. Throw out all the mess and replace it with the 'top of the line' thought process. The gesture that your whole body maintains is that of opening up all the clogged spaces with the stretching from toes to fingertips, reaching out to all the positive energy around you, complemented with rhythmic breathing. It allows you to absorb abundance of fresh oxygenated air into every cell and tissue filling every nook and corner of your lungs.

You may refer to this *asana* in 'The Troublesome Teenage' on page 37-38.

Step 14: Asana 13

Vriksh Asana

(Tree Pose)

When you are all de-stressed and floating, try your hand at **Vriksh Asana**. This one specifically embodies the art aspect in the way you hold the *mudra*. It derives its name from its resemblance to a tree, the true manifestation of human nature, constantly reaching out to energies in and around, above and beyond.

- Stand straight, gently raise one leg up. Join the foot of this leg to the thigh root of the second one on which you are balancing. Let the direction of the knee of the first leg be outwards.

- Fix your eyes at any one point. Let it be your source of support. Keep breathing slow, deep and gentle. When you are sure that your balance has stabilised take a long, deep breath in and raise your hands up joining them above your head with elbows absolutely straight.

- Breathe strong and steady and hold the pose till a count of 15.

- While releasing the *asana*, exhale and bring the hands in the centre of your chest once then lower them down. Hold the bent leg and release it back to the ground. Repeat the same sequence on the second side. Now relax while rotating your knees clockwise and anti-clockwise.

Benefits: This *asana* is extremely beneficial for diverting all the spinal tension away from the central cord. It induces maximum stretching and grace into your movements as well. Even if you have been practising these moves for some time now, just remember the amount of aesthetic value that you can add to them is limitless. So have the ability to look beyond even when you think you have reached your destination because the real growth is in the journey and not the destination.

Once you complete the processing till this stage, you would realise how we have worked taking each layer at a time, first layer activating the energy channel of your spine, and the second layer mobilising the digestive tract. Now we move on to the third layer, which shall focus purely on cleansing the most vital of them all — the breathing channel that forms our life force energy — *prana*.

Step 15: Pranayama

1. Anulom-Vilom

(Alternate breathing)

You may refer to this *pranayama* in 'The Troublesome Teenage' on page 39.

As a word of advice, I would like to ask you to keep your eyes closed during any one of the *pranayama* processes. It would put a stop to all those hassles and tensions, and simply deriving the maximum pleasure of absorbing this fresh, pure, oxygenated air into your lungs. This *pranayama* also keeps your sixth *chakra*, the *aina chakra*, completely enlightened taking your focus and concentration powers to new heights.

2. Vissudha Pranayama

(Snoring Sound Breathing)

You can refer to this *pranayama* in 'The Troublesome Teenage' on page 40.

After doing this *pranayama*, relax and take a long, unwinding breath in. I assure you, it might just feel like the first breath of fresh air you have treated your lungs with, after ages. Also treat yourself with a big broad smile to top it all and move on to next level of *pranayama*.

3. Kapaal Bharti Pranayama

(Pulse Rate Breathing)

At the third basic level of this *shuddhi* sequence, let us get you in-synch with **Kapaal Bharti Pranayama**. It is often misconstrued as being very complicated, but all you have to do is to put your car in reverse gear.

- As you inhale, reverse the movement of your abdominal muscles from the usual pulling of your stomach in as you inhale. You need to expand it as you inhale and pull it in as you exhale. As you do so, let it strike back with a slight amount of force.

- The aim here is to absorb and fill your expanded lungs with all the oxygen, and then in a forceful way, simply flush out all the blockages and irritants. As you start, make sure you go slow and steady, gently building up the tempo as you begin to get the hang of your coordination. You can start with 10 times and go up to at least 30 pulses at a stretch.

- All you speedy schumakers if you have been at it, paying more attention to the number of times you can do this, I will be amazed if you have managed to avert a severe back blunder, an acidity attack or a blackout. I am not against pepping up the speed, but it needs to be complemented with the right rhythm as well or else you will end up puffing and panting with no gain whatsoever.

Benefits: It gives a great pumping action to your heart. In addition, it boosts up the liver functions as well, providing an awesome massage to this fatigued organ.

Beware: Here is an important warning for all of you who have severe back problems, acidity or ulcers. You must not even try your hand at this one till you rectify these problems. Contrary to the popular belief, it might accentuate your disorders. So please do not be in a rush or disappointed! It is just a matter of time before these problems sort themselves out through the rest of the routine and then you can join the club.

4. Bhramari Pranayama

(Mental Vibration Pranayama)

This fourth level of *pranayama* makes you drop all that pressure from the globe over your shoulders.

Please refer to 'The Troublesome Teenage' on pages 40-41 for this *pranayama*.

Step 16: Asana 14

Om Chanting

(Lotus Pose)

You make your way from activating the energy in your spine, mobilising your digestion and cleansing your *prana*. Now for the next level, you head to the level of penetrating and piercing through all the layers that bind you to this materialistic, human existence, and to unite yourself with all that is positive, good and healthy for the mind, body and soul through the chanting of **OM**.

You may refer to Step 19 in 'The Troublesome Teenage' on page 41 for this *asana*.

Step 17: Asana 15

Surya Namaskar

(Sun Salutation)

For *Surya Namaskar*, you can refer to *Asana* 20 of 'The Troublesome Teenage' on page 42-45.

Here I would like to add one more thing that even if you manage to complete 3 to 4 sets of *surya namaskar* gracefully, at a gentle and steady pace, following the entire sequence of breathing, you would be at a greater advantage than

performing the entire *surya namaskar* hastily, rushing through the movements just for the heck of it.

To seal this saga, I leave you with some of the general precautions and techniques you must try to adhere to as you follow the above mentioned routine.

1. Never perform this routine as a matter of regimen just for the sake of going through the motions. You should only follow it the day you truly crave for it because this is the only way it has a chance of becoming a part and parcel of your lifestyle.

2. Never PUSH your body or mind beyond its comfort zone. These set of movements should effortlessly flow through you and never be forced.

3. Always keep your mind focused on the sound and rhythm of your breathing because without the energy flow, these movements would lose their essence.

4. Remember to keep a minimum gap of two to three hours between meals and performing the routine, if you are not an early riser.

5. Try to be as fluid and free in your movements as you can and instil the grace factor from the minutest to the toughest details.

Here I suggest a few parting shots for those of you suffering from the following problems:

1. **Toning up** can be a pretty tiring issue to deal with. To do away with this constant all-consuming pressure, you need to dedicate a little more time to the standing set of *asanas*, which provide more room for stretching. Also, consistently keep building your capacity to perform *surya namaskar*, which is like a one-stop shop remedy. Besides, take due care to consume at least 8-10 glasses of water on a daily basis. Start your day with cleansing your system with a lukewarm glass of water with a squeeze of lime. Be sure to sip on it and not gulp it down. It is the best kick-start for your clogged-up system. In addition, throw in lots of fresh fruits and green leafy vegetables in your diet.

2. **Skin trouble** that bothers most of you at this age is not only due to the hormonal transitions, but also due to the exodus of skin care products that you get inundated with. So I suggest keeping it simple splash tones of fresh water first thing after you wake up and before you sleep. In this twenty-step-routine, focus greatly on the breathing processes and just fill your mind with clean, pure and positive thoughts. Your face simply reflects your mental state of being.

3. **Hair despair** is all thanks to the experimentation mania that hits us at this age. Chemical colours, rebonding, perming, you must have tried it all! It is time to give your poor hair a little 'detoxification'. Get into a regular practice of oil massages, which have a soothing impact on your mental nerves. Olive or lavender oil are most beneficial. In addition, performing *bhramari pranayama* will cure all the disorders from the roots.

4. **Relationship ruckus** is one dilemma we all get hit by while we figure out what we are really looking for. All I can say is never choose the escape route just because of one or two rotten experiences. Take your time to sort out your feelings, maintain your dignity and move ahead. Never try too hard to either create or steer any relationship. Learn to ride with the tide — free and uninhibited — this is the only means to your true self-growth. Read the deeper connotation of this *Let Go* state that exists in each and every aspect of yoga.

5. In case of **Career crisis**, there is no need to fret and crumble under the pressure. Just learn to decipher the sound of your inner voice. As wacky as it may sound, you will be blessed if you manage to do so without falling prey to societal and parental pressure. Meditate on your true aspirations and desires, fuel

your thought process with strength of conviction and carve out your heartfelt path.

Hope these little tips that I shared with you can help you tide over the transition smoothly, helping you define your real purpose of being who you are. All I have tried is to help you read the hidden signs that exist at the physical, mental and spiritual levels that we often choose to ignore, getting caught in the routine rush and ruckus.

The Whirling Working Years

Let us just say that the hardcore joyride of life begins right from here. Personally I feel that it is the most amazing phase of life for women who choose to pursue their careers and prove their professional prowess. Having gone through the rigmarole of first qualifying for professional courses, then digging your heels in to make sure you do not get left behind in the rat race, you finally arrive at the destination. Alas, this is not the end because the uphill task is yet to start as you begin to strive to make your mark, through the cut-throat and chaotic competition.

So for those of you who felt 'driven' by a sense of carving out your own path, and travelling the road less travelled, I dedicate this section exclusively for you. I sincerely hope to help you take the next leap and soar higher into the skies of your dreams and desires. Because it is not enough to have just the ability and excellence! To be endowed by a certain degree of effortlessness is equally essential. This means you need to have an ability to operate efficiently and meticulously, without applying force or pressure either on your physical, mental or emotional being.

When you start working, you will notice that it is easy to fall into the 'rut' of this mechanical and monotonous routine. Soon you lose sight of the aims that you actually set out to achieve, because the strain of living the clockwork-precision life drains you of all your enthusiasm and excitement, reducing the job to a mere means of earning the 'moolah'. The price you pay in turn is losing yourself in this vicious circle. So my aim here is to help you devise a set of remedies. These remedies will not only give an impetus to your professional performance, but also enrich you personally, bringing you closer to the vision that you set out to achieve each and every single day.

First and foremost I would advise you to follow this routine fully or partially, depending on how much time you can spare early in the morning. I, categorically, say morning time due to two reasons. For one, it will cleanse your system giving you the perfect kick-start and boost which will last you all day long, thereby enhancing your concentration and energy levels. Secondly, I know that by the time you get back from a full day's work, the last thing you want to do is exert yourself.

However, there is no hard and fast rule that I want you to adhere to. You can try different permutations and combinations to fit in as and when you manage to steal some time in the day. I feel that if yoga seems like a punishment then you will not be able to derive any benefits from it. So enjoy the whole process. Let it be the ultimate treat for your mind, body and soul.

There are basically **two schedules** that you can choose from depending upon the time you can manage to steal each day in your rushed routines.

Half an hour schedule

This includes the **basic** format of warming up, breathing, stretching, *pranayama*, *surya namaskars*, *asanas* and *Om* chanting. This schedule is to be followed only on days when you are on a jam-packed, fully booked routine. It will make sure that even though you are in a rush, you have set your digestion, breathing and spinal energy in a rhythmic balance.

One hour schedule

This schedule includes the detailed **in-depth format**. All the first schedule aspects, as well as additional *asanas* and relaxation processes are included in this. Ideally, you should set out to follow this schedule each day, provided that your mind is at peace and not rushed or tied down. This schedule is the real deal since it goes a step further in cleansing and balancing you mentally, physically and spiritually.

1. THE HALF AN HOUR SCHEDULE

This one goes out especially to all of you who would have instinctively chosen the short and sweet schedule off the two. But I would rather have you at least give it a shot. These small steps will eventually see you taking the **big leap**. This might also prove to be an eye-opener for those of you who tried making yoga a part of your routine, but could not manage for some reason or the other. So let us start by breaking it down to the basics.

Step 1

Before starting this schedule, your frame of mind should be calm, uncluttered and you should be surrounded by a serene and open space, just about enough to help you be all by yourself, far from the maddening crowds. This does not necessarily mean that you have to own those sprawling acres, or check yourself into one of those fancy rejuvenation resorts. What I am referring to is just the serenity and openness of your mind, body and soul, which you can acquire even in the calm and quiet of your own house. All you need to remember is to make some room for fresh air.

- Start by simply stretching out every single joint, muscle, limb and ligament as you inhale and exhale thoroughly. Keep in mind the basic principle of expanding your lungs and abdomen muscles as you breathe in and contract them as you breathe out. Let the fresh oxygenated air stream right from your toes till the fingertips.

- As you absorb all this fresh energy, it is time to *Warm-up*. Stand with your legs at a distance. Raise both your hands straight up as you take a deep long breath in. Stretch as much as you can and gently begin a clockwise circular movement of the hands and upper body. As you exhale, lower the torso and hands down till the ground. Wait for a split second, inhale and in a circular motion raise yourself up, back to the upward stretch. Repeat the movement three times, making sure you prolong the breathing while coordinating it with your movements. The main aim is to initiate movement into the spine, which is why the legs are kept absolutely straight and fixed in one position. Repeat the same in an anti-clockwise motion three times and you are ready to go further.

Step 2: The Prayer

It is one of the most essential ingredients to make sure that you orient all your energies and channelise them in a positive direction. This is because the words that you utter with a strong sense of faith, belief and conviction possess a certain power to heal all your imbalances. So it is very important for you to fully understand the meaning of the prayer because only then you can connect with the power that these words possess. I often feel this is one aspect that most practitioners tend to overlook. The prayer thus is treated merely as a ritual performed mechanically as a heavily loaded jargon of twisted Sanskrit words.

- So this time, let us try the 'prayer with a twist' and unravel its true essence. Sit in a comfortable pose, totally at ease without any restlessness or hasty thoughts. Disengage from the routine events, close your eyes, fold your hands in the centre of your chest near the *anahata chakra*. With feelings of love, acceptance, trust, faith and belief begin your prayer —

"KARAGAREY VASATEY LAKSHMI (luck at my fingertips) *KARAMADHEY SARASWATI* (wisdom in the middle) *KARAMOOLYA STHITH GAURI* (valour in my palms) *PRABHATEY KARA DARSHANAM* (I look at my hands each morning and get charged to face my day)."

- The reason why I chose this particular prayer is because I believe that each one of us has been blessed with our individual share of luck, wisdom and valour. These are the aspects that set each one of us apart and make us truly unique. This prayer is also a reverence you pay to your hands, which I believe are the medium through which your thoughts, dreams and desires are manifested in the world.

Step 3: Pranayama

In this relaxed, receptive, re-oriented mode, let us take the cleansing and rejuvenation of your *prana* (the life force energy) to a deeper level through *pranayama*. What it literally refers to is the channelising of the vital life force energy by purifying the breathing passage through a variety of techniques.

- The very first step is to begin by balancing both the nasal passages, which form the main gates to the route, that lead you right up to your lungs. Basically, your right nasal passage forms the sun channel; it carries abundance of heat energy (*pingala*).

While, your left nasal passage forms the moon channel; it carries abundance of cooling energy (*ida*). The aim thus is to make sure that your system is neither flooded by excessive heat nor by cooling energies, maintaining a constant equilibrium, that is, the state of *sushumna*. It is like maintaining a perfect balance on the see-saw.

1. Cyclic Anulom-vilom Pranayama
(Alternate Breathing)

I have chosen to modify this *pranayama* a bit to make it a little more effective to make sure that you cleanse every nook and corner of your under-utilised lungs.

- Sit comfortably; make sure your spine is straight. Take the *anulom-vilom mudra* of your hand in a manner where the first two fingers are held firmly under the thumb. The significance of this *mudra* is based on the fact that each of your five fingers has a specific role to play in the functioning of your system. In this case, we keep the first finger turned to keep the 'ego' under control and the second finger signifies the cleaning role assisting this purifying procedure.

- Start by simply taking a deep, long breath from the left nasal passage and release gently through the right nasal passage. Keep this one-way flow on till you complete four sets. Be sure to extend the span of exhaling to almost double the rate of inhaling. Hear the sound of your breathing; let it have a soothing and calming effect on your nerves.

- Now keep the left nasal passage closed with your thumb, and only breathe through the right passage, thoroughly in and out four times. Then get ready to rewind the same process. Only this time, inhale through the right nasal passage and exhale with double the patience through the left. Finally, top it up with keeping the right passage closed, and breathe in and out only through the left about four times again. This form of *anulom-vilom* differs from the regular one, since this is cyclic in form.

• As soon as you open both the passages, fresh oxygen streaming to your lungs activates the blood circulation. It recharges your brain cells as well. The main benefit that accrues is that first by activating the left moon channel (*ida*) and then flushing out through the right sun channel (*pingala*), you balanced out the excessive cooling energy. Then by reversing the process, you flushed out the excessive heat energy through your system. Even though on the surface it seems ineffective, but once you get hooked on to this balancing act, trust me, there will be no greater high. This is because not only does a clogged system affect your health but also distresses your temperament and your ability to have balanced and grounded actions in your personal as well as professional space.

2. Sheetali Karan Pranayam
(Moisture Retaining)

• Start by keeping your jaws closed. Roll just the tip of your tongue upwards in a way that it touches the pallet of your mouth. Set your lips apart just enough to let the passage be open and gently draw a deep and long breath through the teeth till it passes through the mouth and touches the surface of your throat.

• Exhale through the nasal passages with double the patience. Be careful not to use the mouth this time. Repeat the sequence 4 to 5 times and keep the spine absolutely straight, while your eyes remain closed purely focusing on the rhythm of breathing.

- This process allows you to retain the maximum moisture in your mouth as well as avoids the excessive drying up of the throat, which is often the root cause of sore throat allergies. The upturned tongue traps all the fresh air by pulling it in and retains all the moisture at the throat surface.

- During those gruelling long working hours, where sparing a minute of your time to even take a sip of water, is quite a luxury, it is the regular practice of keeping your mouth and throat passage sufficiently lubricated, which proves to be a saviour. Interestingly, this technique is what helped most of the *sadhus* and *rishi-munis* endure˙ their exiles and meditation marathons, without access to fresh drinking water, and survive for a number of days at a stretch. So say goodbye to that parched pathetic throat and get all geared up to move further down the drive-way of your breathing '*prana*' channel.

3. Kapaal Bharti Pranayama
(Pulse Rate Breathing)

An awesome remedy for all you stressed out work buffs.

You can refer to this *pranayama* in 'The Transitional Twenties' on page 63.

4. Bhramari Pranayama
(Mental Vibration Pranayama)

Finally, let the cleansed energies resonate through the mental and head nerves. This one works as the ultimate 'stress-buster' provided that you learn the art to just 'let go' for a few minutes to hear the sound of your soul only.

You can refer to this *pranayama* in 'The Troublesome Teenage' on pages 40-41.

Step 4

Surya Namaskar

(Sun Salutation)

Once you are set with the warming-up and cleansing processes, you may begin with the all-encompassing *Surya Namaskar*.

For this you may refer to 'The Troublesome Teenager' on pages 42-45.

Each time you perform a *surya namaskar*, try to do it like a form of dance and enjoy it thoroughly. Let your body flow along the sequence freely and with fluidity. At the end of it all, it is the 'grace quotient' that is most crucial. Let the foundation of each of your actions be guided by a feeling, rather than a logical technical thought.

Let me now introduce you to the next step, that is, the standing asanas. The one thing that you need to constantly remind yourself when you perform these set of asanas is that they are more like mudras. Here all that matters is the degree of 'grace' that you can induce in them when you hold a particular position. It really does not matter how fast you attain a pose or how many times you can perform it. Its real essence lies in its placid and stable pace. So make use of the space around you, explore it and extend it slowly and steadily, leaving that 'corporate buzz' behind before you step into this serene territory.

Step 5: Asana 1

Tada Asana

(The Mountain Pose)

For this, you may refer to 'The Troublesome Teenage' on pages 37-38.

> *Once you are done with cleansing the energy channel and activating the spinal lifeline, let us stride ahead to the 'sitting asanas'.*

Step 6: Asana 2

Vajra Asana

(Namaaz Asana)

For this, you may refer to 'The Troublesome Teenage' on page 35.

Modified version of Vajra Asana

Try this modified version of **Vajra Asana**. Simply widen the gap between your feet placing your hip joint as close to the ground as possible. Make sure that your knees are joined together. Keep the flow of breathing strong and steady. Let me warn you, at first it might cause discomfort, but do not get restricted by it. Let your ligaments get used to the stretching thereby enhancing your flexibility. If you are the kind who gets tied down to your desk at work, this *asana* facilitates the best possible energy and blood circulation.

Step 7: Asana 3

Shashank Asana

(Analysis Pose)

For this, you may refer to 'The Troublesome Teenage' on page 35.

Step 8: Asana 4

Bada Padma Asana

(Lotus Twisting Asana)

All you need to start with is to sit comfortably in the basic *Padma Asana* (please refer to *padma asana* in 'The Troublesome Teenage' on page 41-42.)

Padma asana is an awesome remedy for indigestion and stiffness in the leg nerves, especially sciatic nerve and the main spinal cord.

- Start by crossing one foot on the opposite thigh and the other foot placed on the other thigh.

- Then slowly take one hand around your waist from the back. Try to touch the tips of your fingers with the toes of the foot lying on the upper side. It is not an easy task and might take you months before you can actually manage to bring in this level of flexibility, but let each attempt bring you closer to perfecting the moves. As you do so, inhale, keeping your neck and head twisted in the opposite direction.

- Now change the position of your legs by bringing the lower one up and the upper one down in lotus pose. Twist the second hand around as you inhale. Continue breathing consistently as you hold the pose, till a count of 15 on each side. Finally come back to the normal position as you exhale and gently release your legs one by one. Stretch out and relax.

Benefits: The main benefit of this whole process is that sitting in lotus pose and twisting facilitates the draining out of all excess toxins from the digestive tract. Moreover, the pressure and strain that often builds up with the long hectic hours while sitting at work, is immediately released throughout the spine, joints and muscles.

> *After you are through up to this point just relax and lie down straight on the ground, leaving your body absolutely loose. Make a mental note of all the cleansing, activating and mobilisation processes that have triggered off a whole new energy streaming right from your toes till the fingertips.*
>
> *Get ready to take this sensation higher as we arrive at the last section of your schedule — the Lying Down Asanas.*

Step 9: Asana 5

Matsya Asana

(Neck Arch Asana)

This is one of my personal favourite *asana* for all those stiff-crick neck days. It is fairly simple and to the point, exactly what you busy-bees are looking for.

- Lie down straight and at ease on your back. Now gently taking the full and firm support of your hands under your shoulders, give your neck an inverse arch, placing the top of your head on the ground firmly. Try not to let the head slip too much, although it might take some time before you can balance the weight on your head. That is why the support of the hands is imperative.

- Inhale as you slip into the *asana* and once you have got the grip, hold the pose up to a count of 15. As you continue to breathe gently, get the hands down over the belly button with the elbows touching the ground *nabhi chakra* zone which modulates your digestion.

- While returning, once again take the support of the hands under the shoulders. Make sure you put no strain whatsoever on the neck as you gently release the arch bringing it back to normal position while exhaling.

Benefits: The main benefit is largely oriented towards relaxing the neck muscles and ligaments which are the most sensitive and highly prone to strain. It is a wonder drug for those of you who have to spend hours on the computer or focusing on massive amounts of paperwork. It is also beneficial for those of you suffering from spondylitis or cervical rib disorders.

Beware: Be cautious not to practise this asana on days when you are already in excruciating pain. Learn to work with the body and not against it. Never push yourself in doing something when your body or mind is under excessive stress. It always backfires.

Relax, stretch out your arms on top, your toes in front and take a deep long breath. Move from side to side gently then get ready to turn around and lie down on your stomach once again stretching out as the body comes in full contact with the ground.

Step 10: Asana 8

Nauka Asana

(Boat Pose)

I chose to call it the boat pose because the way the entire body eventually balances only on the abdomen area reminds me of the way a boat stays afloat.

- Start with keeping your chin on the ground and hands stretched out on top. Slowly raise only one leg and the opposite arm up to your comfort level. Also raise your chin and chest a bit, as you inhale. Keep your eyes fixed on one single point as a source of support as you disengage completely from all other routine hassles.

- Hold the position for a count of 15, taking the support of the second arm and leg. While releasing the pose, gently exhale and lower the arm, chest, chin and leg. Repeat the same sequence for the same duration on the second leg and opposite arm.

- Finally, once you have initiated the movement, it is time to raise the bar to the next level. This time raise both your legs straight up. Then gently raise both your arms and finally the chest and chin as well. Doing all this as you inhale, hold till a count of 15. Now lower yourself down patiently, while exhaling.

- The only source of support is your abdominal muscles. Expand them as you inhale and contract them as you exhale. This motion provides the best massage to your liver and overburdened intestines. It also makes your abdominal muscles stronger since they form the main fulcrum for balancing.

Benefits: The main benefit derived is that this massaging movement helps release all the excess heaviness from the digestive system. It also enlightens and activates the *manipura* and *svadhisthana chakras* leaving you free and floating on the tide of life.

Now relax in *vakra asana* with your feet in opposite directions and hands under your forehead. Let any little bit of stiffness that might have built up during the *nauka asana* get drained through the spine, down the leg nerves and out from the feet in opposite directions. You can turn your neck and head on any one side and even relax the neck and shoulder zone. Once you are done with diverting all the stress away from the central spine channel, it is time to turn around on the back and lie down straight on the ground.

Step 11: Asana 9

Sukht Pawan Mukt Asana

This *asana* has an all-encompassing impact on the three *chakras* — the *svadhisthana* in the lower abdomen, *manipura* in the upper abdomen, and the *anahata* in the centre of your chest. You can refer to this *asana* in 'The Troublesome Teenage' on page 32.

- Make sure you relax taking this foetal position once again. Just 'roll' on your back, up and down in a pendulum motion to release any last bits of tension along the spinal cord. As you relax, you become aware of the upsurging energy through the spinal channel, resonating and spreading in every cell and tissue of your body.

- Relax by bending your legs and lowering them on one side towards the ground with both your knees together while you turn the neck and head on the opposite side bringing a gentle twist through the base of the spine right up till the neck, first on one side and then on the other. This would leave no room for even an ounce of stress or strain.

If you observe the pattern that we have followed, you will realise that we began by absorbing abundance of energy from the ultimate source of energy the Sun, then purified that energy further by opening up the breathing passage. Further activated and enlightened this energy through our life-sustaining channel spine, and in turn mobilised the machinery of our digestive system.

Finally after penetrating through all the layers of the physical realm, breaking through the mind barrier is our next and final step.

Step 12

Om Chanting

Please refer to *Om* chanting in step 19 of 'The Troublesome Teenage' on page 41-42.

Having made this final breakthrough, from the 'physical' through the 'mental', you will feel like you have arrived at a serene 'spiritual' state of being. Binding these three threads together is what helps you unravel your individual unique nature and rediscover the real purpose and meaning of your existence.

For those of you ladies who are willing to go that extra mile and dedicate another half an hour of your precious time to this 'art of balancing', these are some additional aspects that you can include in each of the above mentioned steps.

2. THE ONE HOUR SCHEDULE

For the days when you are not that pressed for time, start your schedule in this way.

Step 1: Stretching, deep breathing and warming-up (as given in 'Half an hour schedule')

Step 2: The Prayer (as given in 'Half an hour schedule')

Step 3: The four *pranayama* processes (as given in 'Half an hour schedule')

Step 4: *Surya Namaskar* (as given in 'Half an hour schedule')

Step 5: *Tada Asana* (as given in 'Half an hour schedule')

Step 6

Uthit Vaayu Asana

In its very gesture, this *asana* is the most majestic of all. If done with grace and a free state of mind, it can almost make you feel like you are ready to take off into the infinite space around you.

- Start by simply keeping both your feet at a distance; turn the direction of your feet on the same side, equally balancing out your body weight on both the feet. Gently start shifting the body weight on the forward foot, keeping the knee straight. Bend only the torso forward, as you begin to lift the back foot up. Raise it up to a point where you can comfortably balance your entire weight on the forward foot.

- Keep breathing steadily, your eyes focused on any one single point and once you are sure of striking the balance, also raise both your arms sideways like the wings of a bird.

- Hold the position till a count of 15. Repeat the same sequence while balancing on the second foot; and while returning back, gently exhale and straighten out your spine. Lower the leg and then the arms. At first, you might lose your balance a couple of times. So be sure to add the arms on the side only after you have stabilised the legs. Keep trying to pull yourself back time and again to attain the position each time you fall.

Benefits: The advantage of performing this *asana* is that not only does it strengthen your leg nerves, muscles and the spinal cord, but in addition it also enhances your focus and concentration skills.

Relax for a while after you manage making a safe landing, and before you get geared up for the next step, warm up your knee joints a bit, by placing your hands on both the knees, and rotating them clockwise and anti-clockwise four times each.

Step 7

Utkat Asana

(The Squat Pose)

I know the name I have chosen is pretty hilarious, but there is no other way that I can make it stick in your mind any better.

- Stand straight, and then very gently, begin raising your heels, middle foot and sole till you finally balance yourself on your toe joints. Inhale as you do so. Keep your eyes fixed at one point. Once you are sure about the balance, stretch out your arms and hands in front as well.

- Then at the most graceful pace that you can maintain, slowly start bending your knees without even a single jerk or sudden movement. Also keep your body weight forward as you do so in order to avoid strain on the spine. Exhale as you lower yourself down. Once you attain the squatting position, make sure you maintain the balance on your toe joints only and place both the hands on your knees. Keep the flow of breathing steady as you hold the pose.

- If the balance is stable, gently connect one hand to the heel of the same side and then the other in the same way. Keep the spine straight. Look ahead as you focus only on your own space, cutting out all other miscellaneous and random thoughts.

- After a count of 15, stretch out both your hands in front once again and at the same graceful pace with the body weight forward, start decompressing the knee joints bit by bit, while balancing on the toes. Once you straighten out fully, as you inhale, give one last stretch and release the position.

Benefits: Your knee joints and thigh muscles derive the maximum benefit out of this *asana*. It also stimulates the digestive system (remember the typical 'Indian loo squat'). The pressure that the squatting position creates towards the lower abdomen induces the creation of digestive juices thereby triggering off a healthy digestion.

Step 8: Vajra Asana (as given in 'Half an hour schedule')

In addition, stand on knees and bend back letting hands rest on heels. (It is also called *Ustra asana*.)

Step 9: Shashank Asana (as given in 'Half an hour schedule')

Step 10: Bada Padma Asana (as given in 'Half an hour schedule')

Step 11

Paschimottan Asana

You may refer to *Paschimottan Asana* in 'The Troublesome Teenage' on page 34.

> *Take a break, hang loose, giving a slight rotation to your shoulders clockwise and anti-clockwise. Move your hip joint and legs from side to side.*

Step 12

Titli Asana

(Butterfly Flap)

This *asana* helps ease out the last bits of tension and restlessness from every joint, muscle and ligament. All you have to start with is to sit straight, join the soles of your feet in such a way that the thighs and knees get stretched out in opposite directions as you bend them.

- Hold both your feet firmly by interlocking your fingers around them in such a way that you pull your feet in an upward direction while stretching the knees and thighs down towards the ground. As you manage to create a sufficient stretch, begin flapping your legs up and down in a rhythmic motion.

- Make sure your spine is straight as you continue to flap and breathe consistently. After a little while, you will notice that the continuous flapping motion creates a 'rejuvenating sensation' through the entire system. It is like shedding all your restless, hasty, impatient thoughts in those few moments itself. All you retain is a renewed, relaxed 'new' you, with only cool, calm and collected thoughts and fresh outlook towards life.

Benefits: The great benefit that you derive from this movement is that all the strain and stiffness that tends to accumulate along the spine, gets diverted and finally released from the legs in the opposite directions.

Taking the support of your hands and elbows, slowly lie down straight on the ground, warm-up a bit with clockwise and anti-clockwise rotation of both the legs about 3 times each. Make sure your knees are straight and breathing coordinated with the movement. You should inhale while raising the legs and exhale with double the patience while lowering them down, in a circular motion. Also keep the pace as slow and steady as you can to derive the maximum benefit.

Step 13

Matsya Asana

(as given in 'Half an hour schedule')

Step 14

Hal Asana

(Plough Pose)

This *asana* is the mother of all remedies for your digestive disorders. Simply stretch your legs and hands by the side of your body, and start raising both leg joints together as you inhale.

- Make sure your knees do not bend and you raise the legs at a snail speed taking full support of your hands. After you reach a 90° level, give a gentle push to the legs backwards in such a way that your toes come in contact with the ground.

- Hold this inversion till a count of 15 as you continue to breathe. Even at this point, avoid bending the knees. This *asana* works in two ways — on one hand it provides a tight compression to the abdominal muscles, and on the other hand it brings about a full-fledged stretch in your spinal cord right through the base up to the neck.

- While returning back, make sure you slide back as smoothly as you can. First straighten the neck, then the upper back, middle back and the lower back, all of it while exhaling. Take a split second break at 90° and then continue your journey back patiently lowering your hip joint, thighs, legs, and finally the feet.

Benefits: The main advantage of this *asana* is in stimulating and cleansing the digestive tract of all its heaviness, toxins and blockages as well as giving the ultimate stretch to the spinal ligaments. It also enlightens the *muladhara, manipura* and *svadhisthana chakras* all in one go.

> *Loosen up a bit, and relax the body as you move from side to side. Twist the legs one over the other, with the arms stretched on the sides to release any undue stress that might have built up during the asana, before you get all set to move ahead.*

Step 15

Om Chanting

(as given in 'Half an hour schedule')

Step 16

Shava Asana

(Dead Body Pose)

Let us seal the schedule with the ultimate stress-buster. *Shava Asana* is the best way to de-stress in the least amount of time. All it needs is an ability to dissociate yourself from the mind completely, cutting out all the mundane routine thoughts that sap most of your precious energy.

- Start by lying down straight on your back with a little distance in your legs and arms (palms facing up). Leave the body absolutely loose. Take one long and deep breath, and as you exhale, just 'let go' of all the restlessness, hectic, routine hassles, leaving the body almost lifeless on the ground.

- Begin by easing out the tension right from the tips of your toes to the finger joints, soles of your feet, heels, ankles, up towards the shin bone, calf muscles and the knees.

- As you move further up, feel the lower portion weightless and devoid of all sensations. From the knees further up to the thigh muscles, relax the pelvic bone area, the hip joint zone and finally feel this relaxing sensation ease out the lower abdomen, the *nabhi chakra* point and middle abdomen, while reaching the upper abdomen and liver zone.

- From the back, feel this streaming sensation drain out all the strain right from the base of your spine to the middle up to the shoulder blade zone, further relaxing the neck and shoulders. Let the soothing energy stream further down to the arms, elbows, wrists, palms, till you feel all the tension squeezing out from the fingertips.

- Finally as your entire body is left weightless and numb to any sensation, relax your facial muscles around the forehead, eyes, cheekbones, jaws, mouth and lips. Leave the tongue also loose and try to attain a pleasant expression.

- As you make this complete surrender, feel yourself rising above all that binds you down to this physical human form, leaving behind all the materialistic pursuits, fading out all those judgements, expectations that weigh you down.

- It is almost like an 'out of body' experience, when you feel as if you are floating above your own body.

- After relieving the body of all its physical bondages and negative energy in this free, fluid and floating state, unite your soul with the purest, most positive thoughts, feelings and emotions. Envision this energy as a white light that you begin to pour back into your system and senses.

- First revive your main lifeline, the spine, with this rejuvenating energy from the base till it brims up to the neck resonating through the digestive system and streaming down your legs and arms.

- As you begin to absorb every ounce of this energy, let it activate your senses, making them more alive, open and receptive bringing you back to life.

- Give a slight sensation in your toes and fingertips. Slowly open your eyes. Take a deep, refreshing, long breath as you stretch out and welcome your new *avatar*.

- This seemingly simple task might take you months and years of consistent practice, before you can make that complete surrender and truly enjoy the process. In the beginning stages, you might just run out of patience as your mind keeps drifting away to the mundane routine events. So you have a choice — either you get distracted, fed-up and quit, or you re-orient your energies, redefine the functions of your mind and rediscover your purpose of your existence.

Whichever of the two schedules you choose to follow, fitting your profile, there are some **basic points** that need to be kept in mind.

1. Never perform this routine as a matter of 'regimen' just for the sake of going through the motions. You should only follow it the day you truly crave for it, because this is the only way it has a chance of becoming part and parcel of your lifestyle.

2. Never push your body or mind beyond its comfort zone. These sets of movements should flow through you effortlessly and never be forced.

3. Always keep your mind focused on the sound and rhythm of your breathing, because minus the energy

flow, these movements would lose their essence. So focus on the coordination of each *asana* and *mudra* with the rhythm of breathing.

4. Remember to keep a minimum gap of two to three hours between meals and performing the routine.

5. Try to disengage and dissociate yourself from all the events of the past, and from the impending tensions of the future. Your only attempt should be to immerse yourself into the depths of the present moment.

6. Follow the schedule at least 4 to 5 times a week and notice the phenomenal change not only in your personal health and well-being, but also in your output at work and in your equation with your colleagues. The magical powers shall spread through and through.

Although, I am sure, this schedule will iron out most of your imbalances and cure all your disorders, but there are still a few conspicuous problems that require special attention.

1. Dealing with stress

In this hectic and strenuous environment that has become a characteristic of our lifestyles, stress is simply considered a part of the big-bucks deal. Little do we realise how this blasé attitude has multiplied the stress, manifesting it in a million other diseases.

- The cure lies in focusing more on the *pranayama* with special attention to the mental vibration — *bhramari pranayama*.

- Dedicating additional time out of the schedule to 'Om chanting' is also helpful.

- Perform *surya namaskar* one or two times more than the usual at an even slower and calmer pace.

- Refine your diet regime to a healthier toxin-free one. 'Fresh fruits and green veggies' is all you need to free yourself from the stress-distress syndrome.

2. Lack of energy

If you have been feeling lethargic and listless consistently and if sticking to your routine feels like quite an ordeal to you, then here is what you need to pep yourself up with:

- Make sure that each morning you start your day with getting some fresh air, be it in your lawn, terrace or the park, performing 8 to 10 sets of deep breathing.

- Face the Sun directly as you perform *surya namaskars* at least 4 to 5 times in one stretch. The Sun being the ultimate source of energy instantaneously boosts up your energy levels.

- Laying greater emphasis on the standing sets of *asanas* is beneficial.

- Make sure your food intake includes high energy supplements like protein-rich items, such as pulses, fish and eggs. Cut down excess intake of milk and milk products, and include the fresh fruits and green vegetables to the maximum. This is one aspect you just cannot do without, no matter what the nature of the problem might be.

3. Enhanced mental focus and concentration

To cultivate these powers, here is the perfect recipe for you:

- Dedicate more time to the *anulom-vilom pranayama* to open up and enlighten your *aina chakra*, in turn activating your focus and concentration skills.

- Perform *bhramari pranayama* to enlighten the *sahasrara chakra*, thereby giving you the clarity of vision.

- *Shashank asana, matsya asana* as well as all the standing *mudras* like *uthit vaayu asana, utkat asana, tada asana* would give a great impetus to your will-power, determination and ability to stay focused for long hours.

- To top it all, perform *Om* chanting for at least 10 to 15 minutes in a day to clear up the clutter and mess that tends to clog your senses.

4. Working for long hours

Having to sit like a couch potato all day long can have a drastic impact on your poor little digestive system, which in turn slows down your metabolism. So follow these steps:

- Pay more attention to sitting in *vajra asana* after meals to make sure that your digestive machinery remains lubricated.

- *Hal asana, padma asana* and *sukht pawan mukt asana* should be performed religiously.

- As far as dietary changes go, simply reduce all whites from your diet, include milk and milk products, flour, sugar and salt. Induce salads and fruits instead. It is a tough asking but you will soon get addicted to this fruity-vegetarian way of living.

- Also most importantly, add 8 to 10 glasses of water to your daily regime and start your day with a lukewarm glass of water with a squeeze of lime, and sip on it first thing in the morning. Not only does it flush out all the toxins but also lubricates and shines up all your organs, replenishing their wear and tear.

5. Balancing Act

Last, but definitely not the least, is the balancing act that triggers off most of the chaos and confusion. So if you are getting torn apart in this tug-of-war between the professional and personal spheres, all you need to work on is your disciplining skills. And what better than a daily dose of your yoga schedule to induce the right quantity of discipline, to make sure that you stride smoothly ahead! Remember discipline does not here refer to the fixed ideologies or rigid attitudes. It is the real essence that lies in learning your body language, respecting your individuality and bringing in-synch your mind, body and soul. Being able to bind these three virtues together every day of your life consistently is what I define as **discipline**.

> *I sincerely hope that these little steps that you will take each day will help you glide through the journey of life because each day in itself is a destination... a milestone. So fade out the past, forget the future and put your soul only into the present.*

The Moonlit Marriage Years

The institution of marriage is based on the strong and solid sense of commitment to one's self. Once you achieve this, only then can you dream of reaching out and having the conviction to make this commitment to someone else. As far as women as a species are concerned, we have been genetically engineered for such deep emotions attached with this institution that committing our mind, body and soul to it flows effortlessly. But to strike the perfect chord so that this deep heartfelt emotion translates into an actual harmonious rhythm for the lifetime, we need to start the journey at our very own doorsteps. This requires refining our thought-process and tuning the imbalances finely.

You also have to deal with the pain of leaving your own home and family, to go and reside with complete strangers, where you will be flooded with expectations of building a perfect home and hearth as well as maintain harmonious relationships with one and all. I do not blame you for going through an identity crisis.

But this is precisely where my job begins, to help you emerge from the load of these expectations, judgements and lifestyle transitions, to stay connected with your core.

I have chosen to discuss the ideal **yoga schedule** in this category, under two broad heads.

- **At the Threshold of Marriage** (includes yoga for all you 'engaged doves' to help you glide gracefully through the courtship period)

- **The Post-marriage Phase** (includes yoga for all the 'newly married birdies' and those of you who have been in the grind for a couple of years to help you flow freely through the adjustment-adaptation period)

My aim behind this intricate classification is basically to cater to all the transitory stages under the broader concept of marriage. This is precisely because those of you who are about to take the plunge need to strike the balance, as much as those of you who have already taken the plunge. So let us dig into those heels and get started!

1. AT THE THRESHOLD OF MARRIAGE

All your energies need to be focused purely on stabilising and calming down your system. Right from the apprehensions of departing from your familiar home ground, to the anxiousness of what your future role as a wife and daughter-in-law holds to the sudden crash course in sex education, and finally dealing with the oodles of excitement and sheer thrill of being united with your soul mate. All of it can leave you pretty drained by the end. Since I am sure you do not want to look like one 'exhausted bundle of nerves bride', for the real glow, it is the yoga rejuvenation programme that you need to enrol yourself into.

As your days might be quite hectic with all that shopping and running around to tie up the loose ends, I have chosen to give you a short, crisp, karmic dose that you can fit in any time during the day, at least five days a week. But if your days are numbered, then I would advise you to take up this schedule daily till you hit the 'D-day'. It is the best wedding gift you would have ever received.

Step 1:

Warm-ups

Kick-start your schedule with this invigorating warming-up session to make sure you stretch out each and every ligament, joint and muscle, to make your system more receptive.

a. Lying Down Warm-ups

Let us begin with the lying down set of warm-ups.

- Lie down straight, leave your body loose, totally at ease and in contact with the ground, right from your heels, ankles, calves, knees, thighs, hip joint, spine, neck, shoulders down till your arms and fingertips. Take a long deep breath and stretch your arms up as you continue to breathe deeply. Expand the lungs and abdomen muscles as you inhale and contract as you exhale.

- Bring the arms down by the side of your body. Keep both legs together and without bending the knees, gently begin a clockwise cycling motion. Inhale as you stretch the legs upwards and exhale as you

compress them down. Use as much space around you and keep the pace really steady and slow. Repeat the movement 4 times and then reverse the motion anti-clockwise 4 times. Take a break and give an easy twist to the legs from side to side, releasing any undue stress or strain.

- Take a turn, balance on the side of your body, placing your arm under the head, while you take the support of the second arm on the ground. Now gently raise the leg on top as you inhale. Take it up only to your comfort level, but make sure you hold it up for a count of 10 and then release it at a snail speed while you exhale. Stretch your leg 4 times on one side and then turn on to the other side and repeat the same. Not only does this stretch initiate movement at the base of your spine, but at the same time, opens up the thigh angle, taking your flexibility to the next level.

- Turn around completely, as you lie down on your stomach; stretch your hands on top, bringing the entire length of your body, in contact with the ground. Place your chin on the ground; fold both your legs halfway up, as you gently twist them down on one side. Make sure your knees are together and toes touch the ground, as you exhale. Bring the legs back in the centre as you inhale and twist them down to the other side. Repeat this twist about 6 times and relax.

- Slowly place your hands under the shoulders. Take the support of your knees as you sit back with feet under the hip joint (somewhat like *vajra asana*).

b. Sitting Warm-ups

Kick-off this routine as you continue to hold the *vajra* pose. Breathe deeply in this position to lighten up your digestive tract, as you flush out all the toxins, impurities and blockages with the steady flow of fresh oxygenated air.

- Proceed by stretching out your legs and hold your toe joints with your hands. If you cannot manage the toes, hold the ankles. Try to keep the toe joints bent inwards. Your neck should be straight as you look in front and gently stretch your toes and hands forward as you inhale. Pull them back as you exhale. To make the back and forth motion smooth, do not fix your heels, let them move freely. The main aim here is to give a holistic stretch to your spine, legs as well as arms without straining the neck muscles. At the same time, your stomach muscles also get a tight compression squeezing out the indigestion.

- So you are all set to stretch further, as you sit with your feet soles joined, holding them with your hands interlocked around and knees outstretched. The main emphasis has to be on bringing your knees as close to the ground as possible. This shall stretch the ligaments of your thighs and drain out all the stiffness. Keep a firm stretch with your spine straight and breathe along. Hold this position till a count of 10, ease out a bit and repeat the same about 4 times. Finally, relax as you stretch out one more time, rotating your ankles clockwise and anti-clockwise moving your entire body side to side. Refreshed and relaxed, we move on to the next segment, so stand on your knees and slowly stand straight up.

c. Standing Warm-ups

Let us bounce up with the standing warm-ups.

- Stand with your feet at a distance (about three feet apart), bend your elbows up to the chest level and gently as you exhale bend down connecting the elbow of one side with the opposite side knee. This will give an 'all-in-one' twist to your back as well as your stomach. Just make sure that when you bend down, your knees are straight. Then repeat the same on the other side. Keep a steady breathing rhythm co-ordinated with your movements. Continue this alternate twist for about 10 times and before you come up, place your hands on the ground, look up and then straighten out as you inhale.

- Continue to stand with legs at a comfortable distance. Keep your feet facing in opposite directions, with a firm grip of your hands on the thighs. Keep your spine absolutely straight and as you exhale, squat in the centre. Make sure that you do not bend forward as you squat. Keep the balance mainly on your thighs and knees. Squat down only till your comfort level. Hold the pose till a count of 10, then inhale and come up. Repeat this movement about 4 times, each time increasing your stretch. Remember, squats are an amazing way of strengthening your thigh muscles and spinal cord.

- In the final warm-up action, stand up close to a wall with your arms stretched out and both your hands should be on the wall. Your body frame should be straight, as you begin raising one leg up sideways (inhaling). Hold the leg up as you stretch out the toe, keep the knee straight and then bring it down gently and gracefully (exhaling). Repeat this stretch 5 times on each side patiently, since the impact is amazing, especially for those of you who are aiming at shedding all that fluff and flab on the sides of your waist.

If you observe carefully, you will notice that even the 'warming-up actions' in a yoga schedule are based on the same principles as the *asanas* and *mudras*, which include:

- **Coordinating** your movements with the flow and rhythm of breathing.

- **Maintaining** the same level of grace and stability in your gestures.

- Not pushing your body beyond its **comfort zone.**

- **Enhancing** the will-power of your mind and learning the art of using the mind, instead of being used by it.

Done with patience and understanding, even these simple warm-ups can be transformed into the most effective set of movements to bring you in-synch with your mind, body and soul.

Step 2

Surya Namaskar

To take this alive, receptive energy that you have triggered off with the warming-up, to its peak, here is *Surya Namaskar*. It is a continuum of twelve yoga gestures that helps the purest and most pristine form of energy from the Sun to seep into you. It is a medium of paying your respects to that source of energy on which your life is sustained. So get a new lease of life by renewing and replenishing yourself.

You can refer to 'The Troublesome Teenage' on page 42-45 for this *asana*.

Modified Surya Namaskar

This time, bring a modification in steps 5 and 8 (the *bhoodhar asana*). All you have to do is once you have balanced out in the mountain pose, slowly taking the support of your knees on the ground, then slide back into the *vajra asana* bringing your hip joint in contact with the heels, as you exhale. Keep your arms stretched out. Once again come up on your knees and hands, and lie down flat on the ground. After performing steps 6 and 7 again, come up on your knees and slide back into the *vajra asana* before you take the *bhoodhar* pose again. Continue following the rest of the sequence as it is.

Performing this modified *surya namaskar* will amply take care of strengthening your spine, stimulating your digestion and activating all your seven vital energy *chakras*. These minor modifications are incorporated with an aim of making your

Modified step 5

system respond more actively and to avoid monotony from setting in. All you need to be aware of is not to push yourself. Do it as many times as you truly enjoy it, slowly building up your tempo, or else it shall merely become a 'military camp training programme' for you. Take a break after each set, to make sure you normalise your breathing and heartbeat, letting the energy seep in and penetrate into each and every cell and tissue. The best is to end each set with *Om chanting* at least one time.

⑧

Modified step 8 ➡

⑨   ⑩   ⑪   ⑫

Step 3

Pranayama

In order to internalise this abundance of energy streaming through your system and senses, we arrive at the guiding life force energy process — *pranayama*. Creating the energy is one aspect, but channelising it to cleanse our mind, body and soul is what makes this process form the soul of yoga.

Since you do need all the help that you can get at this precarious stage, I have chosen to give you, one form of breathing to cleanse each segment of your *prana* channel. It starts with the nasal passages to the throat, to the chest and lungs, right down to the abdominal area and finally reaches your mind.

1. Anulom-vilom for Nasal Passage

Please refer to 'The Troublesome Teenage' on page 39 for this *pranayama*.

2. Vissudha Pranayama for Throat Passage

You may refer to 'The Troublesome Teenage' on page 40 for this *pranayama*.

3. Ujjai Pranayama for Chest and Lungs Passage

For a thorough expansion and extension of the breathing passage, we begin *Ujjai Pranayama* (**Chest Inflation**).

- Start by sitting with your spine absolutely straight. Take a deep and long breath while pulling your abdominal muscles inwards. Hold it right there.

- As you continue to hold your breath, pull the abdominal cavity inwards. Automatically, the chest expands. Try to inflate the chest area a tad bit more with your own effort.

- Hold this inflated stretch strictly up to your comfort level, then right before you want to release your breath, first release the abdomen, then contract the chest back to normal, thereafter you can breathe in gently. Try not to take a hasty gush of air in at once. Repeat it three times.

Beware: Do not breathe in simultaneously with releasing pressure from lungs.

Benefits: The main benefit lies in the fact that once you empty out your chest and lungs of any air, you then compress the abdomen like a sponge to drain out all its toxins, at the same time enhancing the expansion potential of your lungs. Finally as you exhale, there is an exodus of impurities and blockages that flush out as well, leaving your system sparkling. It is this sparkle that eventually appears on the surface as the **karma glow**.

4. Kapaal Bharti Pranayama
for Pulse Rate Breathing

You may refer to 'The Transitional Twenties' on page 63 for this *pranayama*.

5. Bhramari Pranayama for Mental Vibration

It is the ultimate surrender you make to your senses; since this might be the only time you can manage in your busy routine to hear your own 'inner voice'. Let it guide you as it begins to pierce through the layers of chaos. While every other event, relationship and phase of life is transient, the only permanent soul mate you will always have is your own inner being. It is what connects you to your roots, so do not let go.

You may refer to 'The Troublesome Teenage' on page 40-41 for this *pranayama*.

Step 4

Om Chanting

For *Om* chanting, you may refer to 'The Troublesome Teenage' on page 41-42.

Step 5

Shava Asana

(Dead Body Pose)

You may refer to 'The Whirling Working Years' on page 89-90 for this *asana*.

After tuning your physical disorders, energy deficits and mental tensions finely, you take the final leap to enter the 'bliss body state', where you simply flow with the tide of life, shedding all your loads and burying all the burdens. I assure you, after this, going through the 'D-day' is going to be a cakewalk.

2. THE POST-MARRIAGE PHASE

This is where your individual strength and substance is actually put to the litmus test. Once all the pomp and show is over, you begin to seep in the multitudinous changes that you are confronted with. This is the time when you most desperately need to sharpen your adjustment and adaptation skills. I am reminded of one of my favourite quotes at this point —

You can campaign in poetry, but you have to govern in prose.

How I interpret it to fit this phase of life is that we all as women wait with baited breath for this one grand momentous event in our lives. Most often we identify it with all those romantic, rosy images that we have built up over the years, thanks to the Mills and Boons and 'Hollywood Bollywood' hangover. Little do we realise that it is not at all a bed of roses. It takes much more than just your looks, your financial status or professional achievements to make a go of this 'tango for two'.

For beginners, letting go of the 'I-me-myself', egocentric curse, followed by the understanding of the concept of giving ample space to each other is what leads to mutual respect. That is when you have laid the foundation for a lifetime of love. This is my definition of a marriage.

The only way you can dream of incorporating these virtues in your marriage is by inculcating them in yourself first. The first step of this journey begins by adopting yoga as an indispensable component of your lifestyle.

Taking into consideration all your time and lifestyle constraints, here is a schedule that I have chalked out exclusively to fit your phase of life. So no more excuses! Since in the beginning of this post-marriage phase, you are inundated with heavy socialising, new relatives, and a new household with a new roommate, getting a grip over your routine can be pretty tough. So here is what I suggest. Let us start with an **alternate day regime** that will include the aspects discussed.

- **Day 1** with a **5-point-schedule** which includes your warm-ups, *surya namaskars*, *pranayama* processes, *Om* chanting and *shava asana* which shall take you merely half an hour to complete.

- **Day 2**, when you can work on a slightly longer **15-step-schedule** that shall focus more on the *asanas* and *mudras* aspect and shall take you almost an hour from start to finish.

Step 1

Warm-ups

From the warming-up sequence that I gave you in the previous 5-point-schedule in '**At the Threshold of Marriage**', pick out any three (that means one warm-up while lying down, one while sitting and one while standing). You can keep alternating between the different warm-ups each time making a different permutation and combination depending on which part of the body you need to work on more.

Step 2

The Prayer

- For the prayer you may refer to 'The Whirling Working Years' on page 71-72.

After calming down totally and disengaging from the rush and random hassles of the day, it is time to move further to the first series of postures – the Lying Down Asanas.

Step 3: Asana 1

Salamba Sarvang Asana

(Elbow Stand Asana)

You may refer to 'The Transitional Twenties' on page 51 for this *asana*. In addition to balancing on elbows, give a further push and straighten the back totally.

Step 4: Asana 2

Sarp Asana

(Chest Up Pose)

Gently turning around to lie down on the stomach, let us get revved up for the *Sarp Asana*.

- Start by interlocking your fingers over the hip joint in such a way that your arms are stretched out absolutely straight and your chin is on the ground.

- Without raising your feet or legs, gently inhale and raise only your chin, chest, and upper abdomen. Keep stretching the interlocked hands without bending the elbows.

- Focus your eyes on any one single point of support and begin breathing. The rhythm should be such that as you inhale, there is an expansion of your liver area against the ground, and as you exhale, there is a contraction. Hold this pulsating motion till a count of 15. This alternate expansion and contraction is what provides a soothing massage to your overburdened liver and intestines.

- As you relieve your system of all its heaviness and impurities, while coming back, gently exhale and lower your abdomen, chest, chin and forehead as well as arms.

- Relax in *Anand Asana* leaving your hands and arms loose on the ground in an upward direction. Turn your head on any one side and then on the other while bending the knee of that same side just enough to drain out any undue strain from the spine, neck and shoulder.

Step 5: Asana 3

Ardha Chakra Asana

(Halfway Inverted Arch)

To shed all that strain that builds up along the spinal channel, slowly turn around and lie down on your back. As you bend your knees and fold your legs, make sure to keep a comfortable distance between the feet (about a foot apart).

- Taking the firm support of your feet, gently raise your legs and thighs, hip joint, right up till the middle of your torso; inhale as you do so. Place your hands at the base of your spine in such a way that the elbows touch the ground providing an additional support to your spine while you are in the inverted arch position. Just be careful not to lift your upper back or neck while doing so.

- Keep breathing deep and gently to let the energy pass through the stretch. Hold the inversion till a count of 10. Right before you release the pose, first lower the torso region, then the hip joint, releasing your hands from underneath, one by one, finally as you exhale just stretch out your legs as well.

- Relax and stretch the entire length of your body.

Benefits: The main benefit of this posture is to de-stress the spine of all the sprain and strain that is bound to build around it, with all the bending, sitting for long hours or simply running around in circles to keep the household in order.

> *Calm, cool and collected, let us move further to the second series of asanas which are the Sitting Down Asanas.* ˙

Relax a bit, as you lower the spine angle, take the support of your hands on the ground and move your legs and hip joint from side to side. Stretch out your neck to release any stiffness.

Step 6: Asana 4

Vajra Asana
(Namaaz Pose)

You may refer to 'The Troublesome Teenage' on page 35 for this *asana*.

Modified Vajra Asana

- For once try a modified version of *vajra asana*. Simply widen the gap between your knees as much as you feel comfortable with bringing the feet close to each other and the entire weight of the hip joint on them. Keep the flow of breathing strong and steady. Keeping the spine straight, hold the pose for a count of 10.

- Gradually bring one knee and then the other back in *vajra asana*, slowly exhale and stretch out both the legs one by one back in normal sitting position,

- Relax and unwind your toes, ankle joints and legs by rotating your feet clockwise and anti-clockwise.

Benefits: The main benefit of this modification is that it brings the heels totally in touch with the hip joint enhancing the digestive pressure. At the same time, the thigh angle gets a wide stretch as well, in turn boosting your flexibility.

Step 7: Asana 5

Shashank Asana

(Analysis Pose)

You may refer to this *asana* in 'The Transitional Twenties' on page 58.

> *And finally, we arrive at our third destination in this journey of revival and renewal with the series of Standing Asanas.*

Step 8: Asana 6

Akaar Dhanur Asana

(Bow and Arrow Pose)

Stand straight and keep your eyes focused on one single point of support as you gently fold one leg from the back in a way that the heel touches the hips while holding the ankle with your hand.

- Balancing your weight on one leg slowly, start stretching out the folded leg backwards in such a way that the knee also opens up a bit. Be sure to stretch your arm to the fullest.

- Then gradually start tilting the body weight forward as you bend a little in front on to the balancing leg. When you feel that your pose is totally stabilised, stretch the arm of the balancing leg side straight up as much as you feel comfortable with.

- Keep a steady flow of deep, gentle breathing as you hold the pose till a patient count of 10. While coming back, first release the arm while exhaling then straighten out the spine and with one last press of the heel to the hip joint, exhale and release the leg.

- Relax the leg that you balanced on with a rotational movement. Finally repeat precisely the same steps with the second side and to top it all unwind with a bit of loose twisting of the spine and hands.

Step 9: Asana 7

Utkat Asana
(Squat Pose)

You may refer to this *asana* in 'The Whirling Working Years' on page 85.

Step 10: Asana 8

Tada Asana
(Mountain Pose)

You may refer to this *asana* in 'The Troublesome Teenage' on pages 37-38.

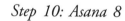

After you are done with the stretching, twisting and turning around, it is time to bring it all together under one roof.

Step 11

Surya Namaskar
(Sun Salutation)

Perform one set of the all-in-one *Surya Namaskar* with the modifications that you tried in the five-point programme of **'At the Threshold of Marriage'** schedule.

Relax and catch your breath as your system and senses begin to absorb this oozing energy into each and every cell and tissue. Peacefully sit down in any comfortable pose, preferably the *Padma Asana*.

Step 12

Pranayama

All the five basic *pranayama* techniques should be followed to cleanse the nasal passage, throat, chest, lungs, abdomen and mental nerves. You have performed them previously in five-point-programme of '**At the Threshold of Marriage**'.

Carry the same vibration that you created in *Bhramari mental vibration pranayama* a step higher making the ultimate surrender.

Step 13

Om Chanting

For the grand finale, we have *Om* chanting. This time set no limits and carry on chanting till the time you start feeling the awesome auras around you. It is not a question of how many times you say it. It is about the depth you say it with.

In a nutshell, here are some of those golden rules you just cannot afford to miss.

- **Quality first, quantity later** — It is only when you have laid down a solid foundation that you can think of increasing the load. Most of us get stuck in the show-off trips and lose out on the real essence of yoga.

- **Use the mind and don't be used by it** — While you are doing an *asana*, *mudra* or *pranayama* process, it is easy to get distracted, letting your mind and thoughts run riot and wander. It is the art of channelising this energy that you create through these graceful movements and cutting out the complex, chaotic, cluttered state of being, that forms the core of yoga.

- **Preach and practise** — Talk, hear and assimilate more and more about this form of art. With each passing day, you will notice how it discretely crept into your way of living. Remember, '**Words are the verbal embodiment of power**'. Preaching will lead to practice which in turn will define who you are as an individual.

- Always keep your mind focused on the **sound and rhythm** of your breathing, because minus the energy flow, these movements would lose their essence. So focus on the coordination of each *asana* and *mudra* with the rhythm of breathing.

- **Keep learning how to live, for as long as you live** — Do not restrict your growth potential by getting caught up in 'fixed attitudes' or 'pre-fixed notions'. To make this journey of life truly worth it, try to become a perpetual student open and receptive to new thoughts and ideas. Shed the scepticism that you are hiding behind and float on the tide of life.

The story does not end right here because I can sense those specific irking issues that you are already or will be facing in this precarious stage of life. So here are some of the major ones that I could put together and the remedies you can find from within your schedules.

- **Hormonal Hassles** — There is no doubt about the fact that this is the most drastic transition physically, mentally and emotionally for us. It is the transition from being a girl to a woman that can take its toll, if not tackled with care and attention. On one hand you have a body that is getting used to the whole concept of sex, while on the other hand you have a mind that refuses to let-go. It is the perfect recipe for disaster. All you need to focus on, in such a situation, is to calm down the system. Get rid of all those mood swings with regular practice of *pranayama*, especially *bhramari pranayama, Om* chanting and a few minutes of peace and solace with just closing your eyes and being with yourself. *Shava asana* would be the most ideal remedy to let-go of the knotted-up emotions.

- **Contraception Chaos** — Popping all those pills only adds fuel to the fire when it comes to hormonal imbalances. First thing is to be able to communicate with your partner and have an in-depth discussion about what modes of contraception you need to adopt and its future implications. The biggest and sole benefit of doing this is that once and for all your mind is put to peace and you have your partner to share your ups and downs with. If you do not learn to relax mentally and calm yourself, it could backfire on your health. So all you need to do is make sure you continue the *pranayama, Om* chanting and *shava asana* consistently. In addition, also perform religiously *surya namaskar* at least 4 to 5 times at a stretch. Be sure to flush out the blockages and toxins by drinking 8 to 10 glasses of water. U.T.I. or honeymoon cystitis is some of the common disorders that temporarily set in during this period. Do not fret. Just feed on fresh fruits and green vegetables. Keep it simple.

- **Weight worries** — As a natural consequence of the above two, gaining weight, especially around the tummy-hip zone is a constant tension. You need to focus on all the lying down series of *asanas*. Increase the duration of warm-ups, and build up your potential for *surya namaskars* to at least 5 to 6 sets. Complement this schedule with a regimented diet including fresh fruits, juices and lots of water. Kick-start your mornings with lukewarm water with a squeeze of lime, sip on it and cleanse your system. Never mix proteins. Never mix rice and *roti* in one meal.

At the end of the day, it is all about learning your body language so do not ignore the slightest signs of disorders setting in, get a grip from the word 'go'.

Serenity Prayer

Here is a special serenity prayer by Reinhold Neibuhr for all you lovely ladies, to smoothly sail you through all highs and lows, pains and pleasures —

> *"God! Give us the grace to accept with serenity, things that cannot be changed and the courage to change the things which should be changed and the wisdom to distinguish one from the other."*

The Precarious Pregnancy

Just around the time when you start feeling all comfy and cosy in the 'wife-daughter-in-law' mould, there comes the bombshell news about your pregnancy.

Now do not get me wrong. Bombshell does make it sound a bit heavy duty. But trust me, whether you planned the pregnancy or not, when the finality of it all hits you, it does take all the patience, prayers and will-power that you have got. It is, without a doubt, one of the most irreversible transitions that you make in your lifetime from being a child to becoming a parent. It is truly in all its essence a rebirth. For a woman, there simply cannot be a more ecstatic experience than this one where life grows inside you, where you become one with the ultimate source of existence, soaring into the skies of motherhood.

Now I know you must be wondering that here I am painting out this holy and rosy picture about pregnancy and there you are dealing with morning sickness, nausea, bloating, etc. It really does not sound all that ecstatic and once you hit the post-pregnancy period, the going gets even tougher. My job is not to scare you, but to simply help you glide through and get a grip over these minor aberrations so that you do not miss out on the ecstasy trip and absorb every bit of this magic potion called 'motherhood'.

> *There is no greater high than seeing your own eyes staring back at you. That little bundle of joy is an undiluted reflection of your own inner being. To be able to see this vision, you need to transport your mind, body and soul on to a whole new dimension of rhythm and synchronisation, which can only be attained by making yoga an indispensable part of your life.*

Break away from the common misconception that once you are pregnant you cannot do yoga. Let me tell you, it is precisely at this stage that you get to taste the real flavour and essence of its most essential ingredients like *pranayama*, *Om* chanting, and meditation, and this is exactly what my recipe includes.

So let's get cracking....

I intend to discuss your ideal schedules under two broad heads —

The Moms To Be
- The first trimester schedule
- The second trimester schedule
- The third trimester schedule

The New Moms
- The caesarean delivery schedule
- The normal delivery schedule

THE MOMS TO BE

For those of you lovely ladies who are in the thick of things, I suggest you follow the *'one step at a time'* remedy.

1. THE FIRST TRIMESTER SCHEDULE

In this very first lap of the nine-month marathon, you need to orient your energies towards getting over the nightmarish nausea, the morning sickness mania, and the hormonal hurricane. I have chalked out a **five-point-schedule** that you can follow, at least on the relatively good days when you are feeling up to it, so that it becomes a tool to help you bounce back on the 'not so good days'.

Step 1

Pranayama

- Start with cleansing the nasal passage with the *'moon pranayama'* wherein you sit in any comfortable position with your spine straight. If it is tough to sit on the floor, then you can even sit on the bed or a chair. Keep your hands in the *anulom-vilom mudra*, that is, first two fingers in under the thumb. Close your right nasal passage with your thumb and begin breathing nice and easy only through the left. Repeat the inhaling-exhaling set about 4 times and relax.

Benefits: The benefit is that since the left nasal passage carries the cooling energy (*ida*) by activating it, the entire system also cools down. Being cool, calm and collected is all that really matters at this stage.

- After relaxing for a split second, start the *'sun pranayama'*. Continue to sit in the same position, the only difference this time over is that you have to keep the left nasal passage closed and only breathe in and out through the right. Repeat the cleansing 4 times and then relax.

Benefits: The benefit this time around is that since the right passage carries the heat energy (*pingala*), it activates the heat energy, enhancing your rate of metabolism, breaking down and flushing out all blockages and congestion.

- Once you are through with striking the balance and ironing out all extremes of heat and cold, let us try to reach the precision state of *sushumna* — where all imbalances cease to exist. All you have to do is perform 4 sets of *anulom-vilom pranayama* (*Alternate Breathing*). You may refer to this *pranayama* in 'The Troublesome Teenage' on page 39.

- Moving from a cleansed nasal passage down to the throat passage we begin with *vissudha pranayama* (*Snoring Sound Breathing*). You may refer to this *pranayama* in 'The Troublesome Teenage' on page 40.

- Next up we have ***Bhastrika Pranayama (Mouth Full Breathing)***. All you have to focus on is to soak in as much oxygen as you can through the mouth and throat passage. So start by keeping your mouth half open and take a deep long breath in. Expand your lungs as you do so keeping the spine absolutely straight as you feel the air touching the surface of your throat. Then, while exhaling, keep the mouth closed and only release the breath from the nasal passage. Repeat the process at least 4 to 5 times.

Benefits: The main advantage is that it helps you absorb double the quantity of oxygen, since you not only inhale through the nasal, but also the mouth passage. It is a booster dose all in one go.

- To complete the *shuddhi* process, ***Sheetali Karan Pranayama (Moisture Retaining)*** works wonder. You may refer to this *pranayama* in 'The Whirling Working Years' on page 74-75.

- Make the final breakthrough with *Bhramari Pranayama (Mental Vibration Pranayam)*. You may refer to this *pranayama* in 'The Troublesome Teenage' on pages 40-41.

Step 2

Om Chanting

As we begin to discover the nature of our true being, here is a medium that shall not only connect you inwards but also unite you with all the positive vibes in the space around you. A true manifestation of the art of healing inside out!

You can sit in any comfortable posture, not necessarily the *Padma Asana*. You may refer to this *pranayama* in 'The Troublesome Teenage' on pages 41-42.

Step 3

Meditation

Make it a regular habit to meditate for a little while every single day. You could start with just a few minutes and build it up to at least an hour or so over a period of time. It is of great value, especially at this tender phase in your life. This is the time you need the insight, the inner dialogue to be able to deal with your physical, mental and emotional transformations gracefully.

- To be able to make this serene connection, you must ensure that you purify your breathing passage and put your mind at peace by cutting out the clutter. Once you have reached this relaxed physical level, you can meditate wholly and soulfully.

- There are no efforts or forceful tactics required, once you have made peace with what you are as an individual and what you believe in. Contrary to the popular belief, where meditation is considered the art of focus and concentration, I believe that it is mastering the art of being free and fluid that defines the true purpose and essence of meditation.

• It all depends on how much time you can devote to just being with your self. Once you get addicted to that, all you will ever need to meditate, is just to close your eyes and take off. So the first step is to make peace with yourself. Only then can you stride forward. No amount of instrumental music or mantras or fixed visions, which are common modes used to help you focus, can make up for the lack of peace within you. Focus, you might be able to build but minus the peace, you will never be able to set yourself free, negating the very aim of meditation, which is — **liberation**.

Step 4

Stretch Out

Stretch out every now and then, especially while lying down. Make sure you stretch out your hands on top, toes in front and breathe nice and deep as you stretch through the length of your body easing out all the stiffness, tension knots and strain. In the mornings, you can gently take a small round in your garden or on your terrace as you stretch out and pace up and down. As you inhale, raise your hands up, and while exhaling, bring your hands down patiently. This simple process helps you pump in loads of fresh, pure, clean oxygenated energy to every nook and corner of your lungs. It also activates the positive energy through your system making your senses come alive. Just be sure not to over-exert your body, since these inception months can be pretty tricky. Strictly follow your comfort level.

Step 5

Massaging your feet and hands

Get into a regular regime of massaging your feet and hands with special focus on your soles and palms, because this is where the roots of all your organs are located. Each part of your soles and palms correspond to an organ in your body. These highly sensitive nerve endings, if massaged regularly, boost your blood circulation which in turn activates your energy levels and mobilises your digestion. It also relieves undue stress or strain which is bound to build up along your spinal channel or neck muscles. So de-stress, unwind and go with the flow.

2. THE SECOND TRIMESTER SCHEDULE

Once you have crossed the first three months, just shed all the tension because you have now entered the safe and sound zone. Even though you need to be on your guard consistently, now is the time that you can enhance your activity just a tiny-winy bit. So this is what I propose — continue following the **5-point-schedule** of the first trimester and add the following steps to make your regime more holistic and healthy.

Steps 1-5

As mentioned in the 5-point-schedule of **The First Trimester Schedule**.

Step 6: Asana 1

Vajra Asana

(**Namaaz Pose**)

Since there is not much physical activity that you can indulge in and your calories have to stay on the upswing, it is imperative for you to keep your digestion mobilised at all times. This particular *asana* is the answer to your prayers. You may refer to this *asana* in 'The Troublesome Teenage' on page 35.

Benefits: The main benefit derived from this particular *asana* is that since the entire weight of your body is lying on the soles of your feet, it initiates fast digestion by applying pressure at that part of your feet where the roots of your stomach, intestines, colon etc are located. I bet it is a revelation for those of you who have been practising this *asana*, who have been told that this *asana* works wonders for your digestive system but really did not know how. Just be sure to keep your spine straight and do not push yourself beyond your comfort level. It is an ideal *asana* even straight after meals (10 to 15 minutes gap is enough) and if combined with sipping a glass of warm water while you are in the pose enhances its impact twice over.

Step 7

Baby Squats

Whether you eventually end up having a caesarean or a normal delivery, this particular posture eases out the stiffness and strain through your spine, neck, shoulders and leg nerves, making the 'D-day' operations slightly smoother. All you need to do is gently stand on your knees, while bending forward just a little bit, place your hands on the ground as well, basically **balancing on all fours**. Make sure you have sufficient padding underneath if you do this on the ground. You could even stick to the bed if it is more convenient.

- Not only does this position balance out your weight proportionally, but also boosts your blood circulation and digestive juices. Most importantly, the stomach muscles get a massage as they hang forward, become stronger and at the same time drain out all the tension and strain. Hold the squat up to a count of 5 and you could repeat it about 4 to 5 times depending on how comfortable you feel.

Step 8

The Butt Press

As the weight keeps increasing, your hip muscles and spine (especially the base) start getting overburdened. So to avoid excessive pain or stress from building up, here is the remedy.

- Lie down straight on your bed. Make sure that the mattress is not too cushy. Gently bend your knees, folding your legs just up to 45 degrees and keep a comfortable gap in your legs.

- Taking the firm support of your hands, press the hip joint down towards the bed just about enough to give a little stretch down to the base of your spine. Repeat this press about 5 to 10 times patiently and without crossing your comfort zone.

- Next time around continue taking the support of your hands and gently raise the hip joint just 5 or 10 degrees above the bed. Also take a strong grip of your feet as you keep the legs folded. Remember to maintain the gap of about a foot and a half between the legs. Repeat the 'butt-lift' about 5 to 10 times again only as long as you do not feel any stress.

Step 9

Leisure Walks

A very crucial aspect of your health drive while in the second trimester, are the daily walks. These middle three months might be the only time when you are allowed to move around relatively more than the first and the last. The first is the tricky inception stage and the last is the tricky delivery stage. Make sure you go for a walk any time of the day, depending on when you feel up to it. Do not bind yourself to a hard and fast regime because being at ease in your mind is what is going to keep your body receptive. Most importantly, combine this light leisurely walk with deep breathing to keep the ration of oxygenated fresh air circulating in your system. Trust me, this is the only time you will be getting to catch your breath before your little angel drives you nutty. So thoroughly enjoy yourself, absorbing all the greenery, fresh air, the chirping of birds and open spaces. Let it be a walk in the clouds. It is also an excellent remedy to cure any sugar problems or liver disorders that might crop up during this period.

3. THE THIRD TRIMESTER SCHEDULE

This is where the real patience test begins. You will feel like your physical, mental and emotional imbalances have touched their peak. This is what I call the rapid seizure of control (R.S.C.) period. Not only do you lose control over the way your body shapes up, but your mind becomes restless and emotions go random. In this state of utter chaos, you simply cannot go on without the cooling and calming therapy of yoga. Even though performing *asanas* is totally out of question, you need to focus more on the aspects of *pranayama*, *Om* chanting, meditation, all of which you have been performing in the first trimester stage. These three aspects hold the key to your balancing act. But besides these, there are additional steps that you can keep handy.

Deep Breathing

To keep your cool and battle all those nasty cramps and contractions, here is the perfect remedy. Sit in any comfortable position as long as your spine is straight. Keep your eyes closed and only orient your energies towards the rhythm of your breathing.

As you take a deep and long breath in through the nasal passage and release it through the mouth with double the patience, your mouth should be in a funnel shape as you release the breath with a little bit of force so as to flush out the hypertensive, clogged-up heat energy from your system. By the end of it, you will be feeling this soothing cool sensation through your breathing passage right from the base of your abdomen till the top of your head.

Body Massage

At this stage, it is not enough to only keep up the hands and feet massage routine but it is your entire body that needs to de-stress. So go ahead and pamper yourself with a therapeutic olive oil massage from head to toe. Just make sure that the massage is soft and gentle and not the usual power-pressure pact one. We do not want you to deliver on the massage table itself. So hang in there and take it easy. You could top it up with a hot water soak in the tub or a hot water shower. It is the ultimate heavenly feeling. So take the plunge and indulge.

I know by now you are wondering how all these steps measure up to being part of a yoga-based schedule. It is pretty simple if you understand, that what I am trying to do here is to give you a lifestyle by refining all those small yet significant aspects of your daily routine that can make your life heaven or hell in this precarious stage that you are in. Coming up next as part of this lifestyle refinement programme are the ideal postures that you need to incorporate consciously into your routine specially while resting or sleeping.

Sleeping or Resting Postures

First of all, always keep your feet and lower legs at a slightly raised level, while you are lying down or even sitting for long hours by placing 1 or 2 cushions or pillows underneath. This simple measure, if followed religiously, can be greatly beneficial in enhancing your blood circulation and avoiding the swelling syndrome. Combine this with drinking 8-10 glasses of water to avoid excessive water-retention, which is a common phenomenon at this stage.

Secondly, make it a point to lie down on your left side most of the times by keeping your left leg straight and overlapping it by the right leg as you bend it a bit. Not only is this posture ideal to drain out the stiffness and tension from the spine but at the same time, it is excellent to mobilise your digestive machinery.

There is no perfect or easy way to go through this **nine-month marathon**. But the least that you can do is to make the ride smoother and more enjoyable and that is precisely where these schedules fit in.

THE NEW MOMS

So you have barely gotten over the nine months saga and boom, there comes the baby brigade. Trust me, even though you are the one who has carried the little angel inside you for this seemingly endless period of time, but to finally hold the baby in your arms is such an overwhelmingly ecstatic feeling, that it cannot be expressed in words. It makes all your troubles, trials and tensions seem so trivial and minuscule. It is like you have finally arrived where you belong. But to be able to keep your sanity amidst all the thrill and excitement, you need to chalk out a routine that helps you recondition your mind, body and soul to this newly defined role of a mother.

1. THE C-SECTION DELIVERY SCHEDULE

First and foremost you need to take at least 2 months off before you can get back to your full-fledged *asanas* and *mudras* routine. So until such time, there is no need to fret. You could easily take up the yoga routine of your pregnancy period. That means you can combine the schedules of the first, second and third trimester which would encompass — *pranayama*, **Om** chanting, **meditation**, **bit of stretching**, *Vajra Asana*, **massages** and **leisure walks**. Even while performing this combined format, be very careful as not to stress out your stomach muscles or for that matter even the spine, which acts like a total shock absorber at the time of delivery. Avoid any kind of unnecessary bending. Just stick to a basic, simple schedule and you will bounce back in no time. Take one step at a time, give your body ample time to recover and heal in its own good time. Do not trouble yourself and your system with expectations and deadlines. The more relaxed and free you leave your system the more receptive it becomes and responds in an active, alive manner.

2. THE NORMAL DELIVERY SCHEDULE

In this case, the only silver lining is that since there was no internal surgery, you can bounce back relatively faster, say in about 40 days or so. Here again I would like to mention that each of our systems is unique and operates at an individual level, so to compare your recovery period with someone else's is totally futile or to have pre-fixed time frames will only pressurise your system unnecessarily. So continue following the same combined set schedule, just lay back and relax.

There are also a few additional precautionary points that I would like you to keep in mind at all times while performing these schedules at your respective stages. They will only spice up the flavour of this sumptuous yoga meal.

1. On the whole, these few tips and tools are just a subtle reminder of the **reconditioning** that you need to deal with at this paradigm shift stage in your life. Reconditioning your thought process, your physical appearance and your spiritual outlook. It has to be a holistic healing process that makes you cherish this new birth in your brand new motherhood *avatar*.

2. For this it is imperative that you **refine** and **filter** in the purest and pious thoughts that shall guide you to the most positive feelings and actions. It shall also make this arduous phase one of the most memorable in your life.

3. Make it a point to offer your **prayers** regularly to that one ultimate source of all life and existence. It could be for one minute or one hour. It could be any mantra or any holy scripture. Just as long as you immerse yourself in its essence and feel focused on the power of the words you say.

4. Instil a strong, solid sense of **faith and belief** in yourself and in your true human potential. Believe in your individual share of luck, wisdom and valour and respect your uniqueness.

5. Never push yourself beyond your comfort zone. Learn to read the signs that your body gives you and get in-synch with its language. Always consult your personal physician before you indulge in any new activity at this precarious stage.

This bitter-sweet experience is what shall truly make you come alive, since pain and pleasure, heaven and hell, day and night, happiness and sorrow is what sums up the true meaning of life, which is a tune of contrary notes and an opportunity of polar opposites. So live it, stumble, struggle, fall and rise through it all. Be like the waves in an ocean, which never fail to rise back once they fall.

The Menacing Menopause

Just like you hit that very first physical transition in your teens, when you suddenly take the leap from being a girl to a woman, this next leap that you take in your post-forties is when the real take-off onto the 'set your spirit free' trip begins. You have surpassed all those adjustments, adaptations, responsibilities, expectations, judgemental years, and finally you arrive at the threshold which I believe is the beginning of a better period of your life. This is the time when you can afford to rise above all other mundane, routine hassles, which you have been dealing with for a lifetime. Now you can finally make the choice to dig deeper into the purpose of your existence.

I am well aware of the fact that it is no cakewalk to go through all those erratic menstrual cycles, mood swings and the bloating accompanied by endless hot and cold flushes. But once you make it through this stormy transition, it is all smooth-sailing. So together let us try to pull ourselves through by following this simple, soulful schedule that shall help you fine-tune and balance out your physical and mental upheavals, reaching the core of your spirit. So throw in all the faith and belief that you have and see the menacing menopause turning into a miraculous menopause. Remember, the schedule that I have prescribed in this section might on a glance seem repeated, full of references to this and that section, but my aim here is not to inundate you with complicated, advanced *asanas*, which shall be a fine display of my expertise, but in reality may hold no practical value for you. So I decided to stick to all that we have already referred to and made a package of only the best (chosen from my first hand experience of working with a majority of menopausal women) keeping in mind your specific age-related constrains. So without giving it a second thought, here we go on this back and forth ride.

Step 1

Deep and Gentle Breathing

You may refer to 'The Troublesome Teenage' on pages 26-27 for deep and gentle breathing.

Step 2

The Prayer

You may refer to the prayer in 'The Whirling Working Years' on pages 71-72.

Step 3

Om Chanting

You may refer to *Om* chanting in 'The Troublesome Teenage' on pages 41-42.

Step 4

Pranayama

In this relaxed, receptive, reoriented mode, let us take the cleansing and rejuvenation of your *prana* (the life force energy), to a deeper level through *pranayama*. What it literally refers to is the channelising of the vital life force energy by purifying the breathing passage through a variety of techniques.

- You may refer to **Moon Pranayama** and **Sun Pranayama** in 'The Precarious Pregnancy' on pages 118-119.

- For **Anulom-Vilom Pranayama**, please refer to 'The Troublesome Teenage' on page 39.

- For **Vissudha Pranayama**, please refer to 'The Troublesome Teenage' on page 40.

- For *Kapaal Bharti Pranayama*, please refer to 'The Transitional Twenties' on page 63.

- For *Bhramari Pranayama*, please refer to 'The Troublesome Teenage' on pages 40-41.

LYING DOWN ASANAS

Step 5: Asana 1

Sarvang Asana
(90° Asana)

For this *asana*, please refer to 'The Troublesome Teenage' on pages 28-29.

Step 6: Asana 2

Hardistam Asana
(Spinal See-saw Pose)

You begin by stretching your legs and gently raising them up to 90°. You must feel a perceptible stretch in your abdominal muscles at this point.

- Once you reach this point, keep your eyes focused on the toes and your mind on the pace of your breathing. Then slowly raise both your arms up to 90° as well while inhaling and also your neck and upper back halfway through, so that the main balance is in the centre of your spine.

- As you hold the pose, stretch your arms and legs as much as you can, as if to reach out to all the positive energy and space around you.

- While releasing the pose, first relax the back and neck, then the arms and finally the legs while exhaling.

Benefits: The main benefit is that it strengthens your spine, since it forms the fulcrum of the pose. It also induces stretching through your arms and legs bringing all your limbs, joints and muscles in perfect rhythm and flexibility.

Step 7: Asana 3

Bhujanga Asana
(Up-stretch Asana)

For this *asana*, please refer to 'The Troublesome Teenage' on page 30 with modification of neck twist.

Step 8: Asana 4

Lying Vaayu Asana
(Lying Flying Pose)

The rhyming name is just to help you correlate it with the movements in a simplistic and relatable manner. Start by placing both your arms in one straight line horizontally.

- As you inhale, raise only one leg straight up, along with your chin, chest, and both arms in one straight line, maintaining the balance on the second leg and entire abdomen. Hold the pose for a count of 10. Keep the same pulsating massage for your stomach, while stretching out the spine and neck, arms and leg.

- While returning, exhale and come back to normal. After a split second, repeat the same, this time raising the second leg and the rest of the body. Finally after

returning for the third time, raise both your legs up, along with the arms, chin and chest. Hold it for another count of 10. Finally relax in the *Crocodile Asana*, that is, feet in opposite directions, heels in and toes out with legs at a distance and hands under your forehead.

Benefits: The main benefit of this *asana* is that it gives an all-in-one stretch to your spine, neck, legs, arms, chest and stomach, leaving you free and fluid for your final take-off.

Step 9: Asana 5

Sukht Pawan Mukt Asana
(Compression Asana)

For this *asana*, please refer to 'The Troublesome Teenage' on page 32.

Once you are done up to this point, it is essential to become aware of how the lying down asanas have a greater bearing on the enhancement of the flexibility of your spine and holistic energy activation, through this vital lifeline channel. However, as we make our way to the next stage of sitting asanas, you will instinctively realise how these set of asanas give a boost to your entire digestive tract, encompassing all your stomach organs and intestinal pathway. Having said this, do not presume that the lying down or sitting asanas are singularly focusing on just one aspect. It is a simultaneous process operating in all the components of the machinery. My aim is simply to help you clear the clutter and focus your energies on one aspect at a time. It makes correlating and synthesising the mind, body and soul seem effortless — which is how it precisely needs to be.

SITTING ASANAS

Step 10: Asana 6

Gomukh Asana
(Double Knee-press Asana)

To accentuate the positive energy and circulation to the next level, let us get revved up with the *Gomukh Asana*.

- Sit straight and bend your legs just up to an angle of 30°. Gently turn one leg inside, towards the hip with the knee on the ground. Then turn the second leg the same way, placing it on top of the first. Try to keep the position of the knees directly one above the other and gradually work at reducing the gap between the knees.

- As you do so, inhale and raise the arm of the same side of which the knee is on the upper position, while you take the other arm around the back of your waist, slowly sliding it towards the upper back zone. Then exhale and bend the upper arm, as you attempt to join the tips of your hands. The arms thus get twisted in such a manner that they provide a stern support to the neck and the upper back area, provided you make a conscious attempt to keep your neck and back absolutely straight.

- Hold the position as you continue breathing steadily till a count of 10. Even those of you who have practised this *asana* before, keep in mind that you should never hold the *asana* at the cost of your posture or breathing, because minus these two, you would just be performing circus antics which are surely not your aim.

- Now reverse the position of the legs as you place the upper leg down and turn the lower one upwards. Repeat the same sequence with the other hand as well.

Benefits: Not only is it an awesome *asana* to maintain a great spinal posture and lighten up your digestive tract, but also works wonders on the thigh-knee area and on the arms and elbows as well, bringing an all-encompassing energy circulation in all quarters.

Step 11: Asana 7

Ardha Matsyendra Asana
(Towel Twisting Asana)

For this *asana*, please refer to 'The Troublesome Teenage' on page 33. In addition, interlock hands.

Take a break because you are surely going to need one after all that twisting around. Just remember, never push yourself beyond your comfort level. If at any point you feel a strain, just ease out the pose, stretch out and then try again. Also if you are trying these *asanas* for the very first time or after a long break, or if you are at the beginners' level, be sure to proceed step-by-step. It might take you months before you can acquire the final pose perfectly.

Step 12: Asana 8

Jaanu Shirsh Asana
(Toe Grip Stretch)

Sit straight with your legs stretched out and place one foot on the thigh root of the second leg in such a way that the knee touches the ground. Make sure your spine is absolutely straight.

- Then gently bend the knee of the second leg in such a way that its foot lies flat on the ground and comes equidistant to the first foot. Now with your fingers, get a tight grip around the toe of the second foot and as you exhale, start stretching this second leg out without letting go of the toe grip.

- Try to straighten out the knee as much as you can, bringing your forehead close to the knee. This one leg stretch provides an amazing stretch to one side of your spine, leg and arm and at the same time a tight squeeze to your stomach.

- Hold this grip for a count of 15 as you continue to breathe easy, then while returning, first raise your face and neck and then straighten out the spine as you take a long and deep breath. Stretch the hands right on top. Now exhale and release.

- Repeat the same sequence with the second leg and make sure there are no sudden movements or jerks while going down or releasing the pose.

Benefits: The benefit that your body derives through this pose is that it helps you bring an all-encompassing stretch to your leg nerves, arms, spine and right from the base up to the neck. Gradually it enhances your flexibility quotient and bridges the gaps between your limbs and joints, making the whole body toned and supple.

Step 13: Asana 8

Vajra Asana
(Namaz Asana)

For this *asana*, please refer to 'The Troublesome Teenage' on page 35.

Step 14: Asana 9

Shashank Asana
(Analysis Pose)

For this *asana*, please refer to 'The Troublesome Teenage' on page 35.

STANDING ASANAS

Step 15: Asana 10

Tada Asana
(Mountain Pose)

For this *asana*, please refer to 'The Troublesome Teenage' on page 37-38.

Step 16: Asana 11

Utkat Asana
(The Squat Pose)

For this *asana*, please refer to 'The Whirting Working Years' on page 85. In addition, touch heels and twist without touching the ground by knees.

Step 17: Asana 12

Trikona Asana

(Triangle Asana)

Please refer to 'The Troublesome Teenage' on pages 36-37.

Step 18: Asana 13

Uthit Sukht Pawan Mukt Asana

(Standing Compression Pose)

Through this *asana*, you can make sure that you release every last ounce of indigestion and impurity from the system.

- As you stand straight, raise one leg right up till your abdomen area. Inhale as you do so. When you feel that you have reached a comfortable balance zone, then interlock your fingers around the leg and press it as hard as you can towards the abdomen and chest. Try to place the grip of your hands in the centre of the shinbone of your leg. It will enhance the compression.

- Make sure that your spine is absolutely straight and breathing is deep and gentle. With every breath you take in, the fresh supply of oxygen, combined with the compression, stimulates the digestion. And with every breath you take out, you release the toxins, impurities and blockages through the system. It is like squeezing a sponge and draining its excess moisture. Simultaneously, your spine too gets an elongated stretch through the leg nerve, making it a two-way remedy.

Step 19: Asana 14

Uthit Vaayu Asana

Please refer to 'The Whirling Working Years' on page 84.

Step 20: Asana 15

Shava Asana
(Dead Body Pose)

- We seal the schedule with the ultimate stress buster. For *Shava Asana*, please refer to 'The Whirling Working Years' on page 89-90.

Some basic points that need to be kept in mind that shall allow you to maintain the highest levels of receptivity while performing this schedule are as follows:

1. **Never perform** this routine as a matter of regimen just for the sake of going through the motions. You should follow it only the day you truly crave for it. This is the only way it has a chance of becoming a part and parcel of your lifestyle and individuality.

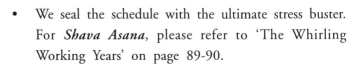

2. **Never push** your body or mind beyond its comfort zone, these sets of movements should effortlessly flow through you and not be forced.

3. Always keep your **mind focused** on the sound and rhythm of your breathing because minus the energy flow these movements would lose their essence. So focus on the coordination of each *asana* and *mudra* with the rhythm of breathing.

4. Remember to keep a **minimum gap** of two to three hours between meals and performing the routine, that is, if you do not manage fitting it in your rushed mornings.

5. Try to **disengage and dissociate** yourself from all the events of the past and from the impending tensions of the future. Your only attempt should be to immerse yourself into the depths of the present moment.

Follow the schedule at least 4 to 5 times a week and notice the phenomenal change in the way you think, feel and act. It will be like a total makeover.

As for tackling some of the specific problems that erupt at this stage, here are some remedies you can adopt. So here is my list of the five top most dreaded syndromes:

1. **The flushes:** One of the most common side-effects of the menopause hitting you full force are the flushes. Sometimes a cold flush and sometimes a hot one! It is the temperature control mechanism of the body that can drive you nuts. So all you need to do is strengthen your combat tools with extra emphasis on the alternate breathing (*anulom-vilom*), *moon pranayama*, that is, only left nasal passage breathing for the hot flushes, and *sun pranayama*, that is, only right nasal passage breathing for the cold flushes.

2. **Migraines:** With all that hormonal upheaval, there comes the deadliest of them all, the migraine

headaches. All you need to do in this case is to pay greater attention to all the *pranayamas*, especially *bhramari*, *Om* chanting, *moon pranayama* and *shava asana*.

3. **Blood pressure:** Once again a direct impact of excessive heat in the body leads to high blood pressure, which can be eased out by regular regimes of *pranayama* (10 to 15 minutes, twice a day), especially *moon pranayama* combined with *bhramari pranayama* and *Om* chanting. For excessive cold in the body that leads to low blood pressure, *sun pranayama*, *kapaal bharti* and *surya namaskars* are of utmost value.

4. **Rheumatism or arthritis:** The only answer lies in consistent performance of *surya namaskars* (at least 4 to 5 sets at a stretch), standing set of *asanas*, especially *utkat asana* and *trikona asana*. Most importantly, you must make massaging a regular feature in your routine (preferably with olive oil). It is the best way to keep the machinery of your joints well-oiled and lubricated.

5. **Thyroid:** Though it is not caused as a direct result of menopause, but it is at this stage that you are most prone to catching this disorder. It is a gland situated in your throat that holds the key to your overall balance. It acts like a stabiliser in your system. So the best way to instil this balance in your body is to pay more attention to the *vissudha pranayama*, in addition to all other *pranayama* techniques and *Om* chanting. Performing *surya namaskars* as well as *hardistam asana* religiously, along with the rest of the yoga schedule, also works as the ultimate remedy.

So go ahead and say 'yes' to life because life simply mirrors your image. So change your face from fear to freedom, from rejection to respect, and embrace your true being while discovering the true purpose of life.

The Graceful Aging Years

After all that has been said and done about your mental relaxation, physical rejuvenation and spiritual revelations, one final aspect that seals all schedules is the **Diet Regime**. Now do not get me wrong. I am not going to prescribe you one of those 'all boiled veggies' or some vague 'only tomato, potato or fruit' based unsustainable diets. This particular generalised diet that I have designed for you is based on the principle of 'Keep It Simple' that truly embodies the essence of yoga — live simple, think simple, and eat simple.

You must be wondering as to how aging gracefully has anything to do with food. Well, this is how it works — your body is like an empty vessel that needs to float on the tide of life. The lighter and simpler the food the easier it is to float, but the heavier and richer the food, greater are your chances of drowning. It is the purity of your eating that shall determine the purity of your living. So if you want to be one of those graceful oldies 'living up' every moment minus the signs of aging or a fatigue-driven life, here is the lifetime diet for you.

There are **two aspects** that need to be kept in mind while following this diet, one is the time frame and the other is the sequence frame.

1. **Early Morning (6:30 a.m.-7:30 a.m.):** Start with a glass of water and then have a lukewarm glass of water with a squeeze of half or full lemon. Make sure you sip the warm water slowly and patiently. Not only does the warm water break down all the undigested fats, but the squeeze of lime flushes out the toxins further, shines up all the organs and greatly boosts up your immunity system as well.

2. **Breakfast (8:30 a.m.-9:30 a.m.):** Either you have a glass of fresh fruit juice, followed by a bowl of oats/porridge/flakes/suji/one boiled egg with one whole

wheat bread slice or you can have a bowl of freshly cut fruits (any two at a time; try to avoid excess of the sweeter tasting fruits like mangoes, grapes, chikoos, dates etc. and focus more on papaya, apples, watermelon etc.), followed by one medium glass of milk. You could also go for a nice cup of brewed tea without sugar. It will be tough to begin with, but trust me, once you get into the habit, you would not want it any other way. It is the healthiest for your system, since you do not boil the tea leaves; you retain their 'herbal' quality.

3. **Lunch (12:30 p.m.-1:30 p.m.):** Kick-start your meal with a big bowl of crisp and crunchy salad. Add all the possible greens that you can lay your hands on, right from cucumber to lettuce to cabbage to mint leaves. Up next, have one medium bowl of either a vegetable or a *dal*, along with 2 medium-sized chapattis. You could have a small bowl of curd as well and if you have to then add brown sugar instead of white.

4. **Early Evening (3:30 p.m.-4:30 p.m.):** You could either have a medium glass of salty buttermilk (*lassi*) in which the proportions of curd to water are 1:3, means three times the amount of water as the curd. You may also have a cup of brewed tea without sugar with only 7 to 8 drops of milk. With this choice of drinks, you could add either a whole wheat biscuit or you could have one fresh *amla*. You do need to have acquired taste for this because it might taste horrendous to begin with. But trust me, it is one of the richest sources of vitamin C, almost 16 times more effective than even lemon. You really do not want to miss out on this one.

5. **Dinner (7:30 p.m.-8:30 p.m.):** This time too, attack the salad section. You could make many sustainable

combinations. One such combination is that of a corn, tofu salad or sprouts with fresh lemon juice. If the meal is Indian, then have another bowl of vegetable or *dal* depending on what you had for lunch. You can alternate and balance out the meal. Take care not to keep having only *dals* for both the meals. Take them with one medium-sized chapatti or a bowl of rice.

If the cuisine is continental, then you can opt for salads, baked vegetables, grilled or roasted fish with a slice of whole wheat bread.

Make sure you seal the hunger pangs around this time at least for the weekdays. You can freak out and play around with your diet a bit on the weekends. Also make it a point to never mix your chapattis with rice. Never have water between the meals, unless you are choking on your meal. But during the day be sure to consume at least 8 to 10 glasses of water in the entire day.

The aim here is not to make you feel miserable even though the first few days of following this routine might do so. The real aim is to recondition and refine your eating habits slowly and steadily to a point where you truly eat to live and not live to eat.

The mantra is simply 'think before you open your mouth' not only to measure your words, but also to measure your food. Both if left unchecked can create all the possible chaos and disorder in your life.

You can take as much time as you like to fall in line with this routine, just as long as you feel happy doing it. From my side, I assure you the peach of health, peak of energy and pounds of loss of weight.

So *Bon Appetite,* ladies.

Four Pillars of Yoga

*A*t the end of this awesome journey that I have undertaken with you, passing through all your multitudinous transitions and phases, I leave you with some very basic yet very essential concepts. These concepts form the four pillars of yoga and serve as a discipline which shall guide you further. The journey must go on deeper and deeper till you reach the core of your inner being. The day when you are completely at peace with who you are and what you are blessed with, that shall be your destination. Until such time, these are your pillars of finding the purpose of your being.

1. *Karma:* Central to the philosophy of yoga, this is the **universal spiritual concept** of reaping what you sow.

2. *Kleshas:* These are **afflictions** which distort our mind and our perception. They affect how we think, act and feel. They create suffering, binding us to the endless cycle of birth and rebirth, preventing us from achieving enlightenment.

3. *Koshas:* Imagine them as **layers** of an onion forming a barrier, preventing us from realising our true nature of bliss. Yoga is the tool to peel back these layers to bring our awareness deeper.

4. *Moksha* and *Maya:* This is the state of **liberation** and freedom, a state of non-ego where the self vanishes and one stands free from all desires.

In the end, I thank you for having the patience to have gone through my book which holds the essence of yoga. I only hope that in my small, minuscule way I have managed to give you that 'wake-up call' that we all require from time to time. I sincerely feel blessed to have been able to put forth my experiences and share my vision with each one of you. Here is a thought that I leave you with that has been the most inspiring guiding force for me. I hope it will take you as well from strength to greater strengths.

> *"When you are inspired by some great purpose and some extraordinary project, then all of your thoughts break their bond. Your mind transcends limitations, your consciousness expands in every direction, and you find yourself in a new, great and wonderful world. Dormant forces, faculties and talents become alive and you discover yourself to be a greater person by far than you ever dreamed yourself to be."*

— **Patanjali**

Index

Pregnancy made comfortable with Yoga & Dietetics

*T*his unique and must read book by Nishtha Saraswat is the only one of its kind that deals with pregnancy related problems with the help of unique combination of yoga and dietetics, two of the most relevant subjects in today's social context.

The effort has been put behind understanding various stages involved in pregnancy in a simple and easy to understand manner. The stress has been laid on providing practical solutions to the common problems faced by women before, during and after pregnancy. A combination of yogic exercises, meditation and special menu plans has been recommended keeping in mind the needs of Indian women.

The book has been divided into various sections for ease of reference. The extensive use of pictures, tables, illustrations and testimonials lends practicality to the book and makes it user-friendly. The book aims at becoming a complete reference manual during the journey from planning pregnancy to getting back in a healthy shape post pregnancy. Aspiring mothers will find this book indispensable in their daily lives.

Regular reference and usage of the book during pregnancy will ensure that pregnancy becomes a comfortable and pleasant experience for all women.

Nishtha Saraswat

A complete reference book covering all stages from Pre-pregnancy to Post-pregnancy

Big Size • Pages: 132
Price: Rs. 150/- • Postage: Rs. 15/-

Yoga for Health & Personality

$\mathcal{Y}$oga is a holistic science promoting specific techniques for integrated development of man's entire being — physical, mental, emotional and spiritual. Regular practice of yoga ensures sound health, sharp intellect, youthful looks, abundant energy, emotional maturity, composure, compassion and spiritual awareness.

This book is an unmatched work that explores all practical aspects of yoga — Asanas, Pranayama, Shat Karma and meditation. The pages are profusely illustrated with photos of yogic asanas performed by the author and others, making them easy to follow. The step-by-step guidelines explaining the techniques for every posture. The specific benefits of each asana are also stated. Suitable for young and old alike, just half an hour of daily yoga will help you overcome bad habits, improve your personality and make you a better human being in every respect.

Dr G. Francis Xavier, Ph.D

Big Size • Pages: 124
Price: Rs. 96/- • Postage: Rs. 15/-

N.S. Ravishankar

$\mathcal{Y}$oga today is universally acknowledged as a natural way to sound health and overall physical and mental well-being. And given its popularity, a variety of self-help yoga guides are available to the reader. But what makes this book unique is its approach and presentation. The book packs over 100 yogic asanas thoroughly illustrated, and backed by well-designed techniques to perform specific exercises from the first step to the last with each explanation supplemented by the therapeutic advantages of that posture. From how Tadasana gives strength to legs and feet and stimulates nervous system, Garudasana removes cramps in calf muscles, Natarajasana helps to reduce fat, it goes on to explain the benefits of Ardha Chandrasana in strengthening digestive system, and of Vatayanasana in curing joint pain, to list a few.

In addition, the book offers an overview of this age-old science, besides a detailed index of different ailments and the names of asanas useful in curing them. A special chapter is also devoted to specific yogic exercises for Farmers, Pregnant women, Aged people, Artists and Craftsmen, Models, Students, Executives and Sportsmen.

Big Size • Pages: 184
Price: Rs. 120/- • Postage: Rs. 15/-